THE CHERRY ORCHARD

Anton Chekhov

THE CHERRY ORCHARD

A re-imagining by Gary Owen

OBERON BOOKS
LONDON

WWW.OBERONBOOKS.COM

First published in 2017 by Oberon Books Ltd
521 Caledonian Road, London N7 9RH
Tel: +44 (0) 20 7607 3637 / Fax: +44 (0) 20 7607 3629
e-mail: info@oberonbooks.com
www.oberonbooks.com

A catalogue record for this book is available from the British
Library.

PB ISBN: 9781786823045
E ISBN: 9781786823052

Cover image: Burning Red

In memory of Jimmy and Megan Owen.

Acknowledgements

Though I am old enough to hazily remember the late 70s and early 80s, Andy Beckett's books *Promised You a Miracle: Why 1980-82 Made Modern Britain* and *When The Lights Went Out: Britain in the 70s* were invaluable in reacquainting me with facts.

Thanks to Nicola Reynolds, Suzanne Packer, Steffan Rhodri, Leila Crerar, Morfydd Clark, Gwawr Loader, Francois Pandolfo, Keiron Self and Matthew Bulgo for showing me Chekhov during the initial development days at the Sherman Theatre.

Thanks to Emily McLaughlin, Nina Steiger and all the National Theatre Studio for an incredibly productive development week. And thanks especially to Kate Harper, Roseanna Frascona, Leila Crerar, Mateo Oxley, Trevor Fox, Isabella Nefar and Mark Arnold for digging into the script with such enthusiasm and generosity, often before seven hours of being angelic in America.

Thanks to Rachel O'Riordan, Julia Barry, and every single member of staff at the Sherman Theatre for your absolute commitment to creating a thriving, ambitious theatre for all the people of Cardiff and our country. Diolch o ddwfn calon.

And thanks to my dad, for local colour.

Notes on dialogue and accent

Words in [square brackets] are not to be spoken, but are included to clarify intent.

Words in {curly brackets} are asides included for texture and rhythm, and can be thrown away or omitted entirely.

A forward slash in a line indicates the point at which the next speech begins.

RAINEY was brought up in London, and retains, as GABRIEL does, in general an upper-middle class English accent. However she pronounces Welsh names accurately – so for example she pronounces 'Alun' as 'Alin', rather than Anglicising it to 'Alan'.

Her daughters, though raised in Pembrokeshire, have inherited their mother's accent with just the odd local inflection. But they too pronounce local names as would locals – so Haverfordwest is 'Ha'fordwest', Slebech is 'Slebbidge'.

DOTTIE, LEWIS and CERI are local.

ONE

The sea. The Atlantic. A moonlit night. Wave after wave after wave crashes against the shore.

And then we move. East, inland.

A river running to the sea splashes over pebbles.

Wind whips between sand dunes, shakes sea grasses.

We follow the river off the coast into woodland.

The gurgle of water, the creak of branches, the rustle of leaves.

Badgers bundle through undergrowth. An owl calls.

Out of the forest, onto farmland. Pasture. Sleeping cows snuffle. In the distance, a diesel train flashes past.

Across the fields, into a long kitchen garden. Into the kitchen.

A broom on a cool tile floor. A half-hummed tune. Crackle of a fire. The tick of a clock.

The room tone grows, grows – there's a hazy medium wave radio, the beeps of the Radio 4 time signal and –

– a living room.

ALUN LEWIS fast asleep stretched out on a sofa. Dressed for outdoors. Work boots, up on the arm.

DOTTIE comes on, bringing glasses and wine. Walks to a table, busies herself putting out the glasses, opening the wine, putting a tea towel around it.

DOTTIE: *(As she works.)* Lew, they're coming.

LEWIS doesn't respond.

DOTTIE: Oi.

Doesn't respond.

DOTTIE: OI!!!

He maybe snores.

DOTTIE stops what she's doing. Goes over to him – takes in his boots on the sofa, is annoyed by that.

Jabs him.

LEWIS: Yes but you won't, you won't...

LEWIS turns over.

DOTTIE glares at him.

Turns, goes.

LEWIS: There's a good little...

DOTTIE returns with a lipstick. Opens it. Pops out the stick.

Leans in and applies it daintily to LEWIS's lips.

Stands up, pops the top back on the lipstick, puts it neatly away in a pocket.

Then grabs LEWIS's feet, drags them off the sofa, lets them fall to the floor.

LEWIS: Never! Not even once!

DOTTIE stares at him.

LEWIS: What?

DOTTIE: Make yourself at home, why not.

LEWIS recovers instantly.

LEWIS: That's what you / told me to –

DOTTIE: You were asleep! Dirty boots up on my settee...

LEWIS: *Your* settee?

DOTTIE: I'll be the one cleaning it up.

LEWIS: I was resting my eyes.

DOTTIE: – resting the bloody lot of you.

She smiles at him.

LEWIS: I was *not* asleep.

DOTTIE: Oh okay.

She just touches her lips, as if doing it without thought.

DOTTIE: I'll fetch the dustpan and brush. You're hardly going to.

DOTTIE marches off.

LEWIS gathers himself.

There's something not right.

He puts his finger to his lips, rubs.

Inspects his finger, not quite sure –

– then realises what he's looking at.

Looks after DOTTIE.

And immediately she returns.

DOTTIE: What?

LEWIS hides his finger as if it's somehow incriminating.

LEWIS: Nothing.

DOTTIE: Such an old man thing to do. Falling asleep everywhere.

She's walking towards the sofa with dustpan and brush. Stops.

DOTTIE: *(To herself.)* {No, hold on –}

She diverts, heads to the table, puts pan and brush on the floor, pours wine.

LEWIS: Shouldn't pour the wine till they're actually here, it gets warm.

DOTTIE: They are here.

LEWIS: They're never?

LEWIS leaps up, straightens himself out. Fiddling with his tie.

DOTTIE: I did say. Perhaps you didn't hear, wonder why.

GABRIEL enters, bearing flowers.

GABRIEL: Hello all!

DOTTIE: *(To LEWIS, re his tie.)* You're making that worse.

LEWIS: Can you [fix it]?

DOTTIE: Yes, why not...

DOTTIE puts down the bottle she's pouring from, goes over, fixes his tie.

3

GABRIEL: I wandered through the garden, picked flowers. Will she like flowers?

DOTTIE: I'm sure she'll love them.

GABRIEL: People do, don't they? In general. Still this is my sister.

GABRIEL holds out the flowers to DOTTIE.

She comes over, takes them.

GABRIEL: Alan. How are you.

LEWIS: As can be expected.

GABRIEL: Looking a little…

He just glances at LEWIS's lips. LEWIS picks it up.

LEWIS: What?

GABRIEL: Flustered.

DOTTIE: He conked out on the settee.

LEWIS: *(Of his tie.)* You've done this so I can only just breathe!

DOTTIE: I'll come and tighten it in a sec.

DOTTIE heads off with the flowers.

GABRIEL: Not to worry, I do that all the time.

LEWIS looks, baffled.

GABRIEL: Fall asleep. Anywhere and everywhere. Sometimes mid-conversation. It comes with age, I'm afraid.

LEWIS: I did not fall asleep!

GABRIEL: The other thing I find? Toilet activities. I go to see the proverbial man about the proverbial, you know, and I think I've finished and then – five minutes later, I have to go again. And it's not just a few drops. It's decent widdle in itself. It's like the muscles don't have the strength anymore –

DOTTIE returns, flowers in a vase.

GABRIEL: Did you cut the / stems –

DOTTIE: *(Cutting in.)* Yes, I cut the stems.

GABRIEL: On the diagonal?

She stares at him.

DOTTIE: But of course.

GABRIEL: Good girl. So as I say –

GABE's taking off his coat. DOTTIE puts vase down, goes to pick up dustpan and brush, walks towards sofa, stops, goes back to table, puts down dustpan and brush, picks up wine bottle, is about to pour when she notices GABE is holding his coat out to her, takes his coat, drapes it over her arm, picks up bottle again, pours –

GABRIEL: – it's as if the muscles that pump your wee out – *(To DOTTIE.)* Is that cold enough?

DOTTIE: Should be, I've had it next to my heart all night –

GABRIEL doesn't get it. Then does.

GABRIEL: Ah, very good.

LEWIS picks up the glass she's poured.

DOTTIE: Help yourself Lew.

LEWIS: Sorry, I thought they were –

GABRIEL: – the muscles don't have the strength any more to get a whole wee out in one go. I have to trot back for a second stab five minutes later.

DOTTIE stops what she's doing, stares at him.

GABRIEL: Sorry. Not really talk for a lady.

LEWIS: She's hardly a lady, so…

DOTTIE: And if you'd grown up in house, not a cowshed, you'd know to wipe your feet when you come in. *(To GABRIEL.)* No the reason I [stopped] – you were talking about –

GABRIEL: – urination. I do apologise.

DOTTIE: And it takes you a couple of goes? To get it all out?

GABRIEL: Age doesn't come alone, they say. Whoever they might / be…

DOTTIE: *(Over him.)* Gabriel, I don't think that's age. Joking aside now.

GABRIEL: What on else could it be?

DOTTIE: My uncle, he went like that. And the doctors said, that was the first sign.

GABRIEL: Sign of what?

DOTTIE: The big… you know.

GABRIEL: The big?

DOTTIE: *(Elaborately mouths it.)* Cancer.

GABRIEL: What?

LEWIS: I think she said *(Mouths.)* cancer.

GABRIEL: *(Mouths it back.)* Cancer?

DOTTIE nods.

GABRIEL: Cancer?

DOTTIE: Yeah.

GABRIEL: Of the…

Points down towards his crotch.

DOTTIE: Of the willy, that's right.

GABRIEL: Oh my goodness…

DOTTIE: They said once you get to that stage, when you're needing two wees –

She pauses – he's held.

GABRIEL: What?

DOTTIE: It's too late.

GABRIEL: Oh my goodness. Oh my goodness me.

DOTTIE stares at him – then breaks.

DOTTIE: Not really!

GABRIEL: *What?*

DOTTIE: Had you though didn't I? It's not cancer. You're just bloody old.

GABRIEL: You were joking?

DOTTIE: Yeah.

GABRIEL: But you said, joking aside.

DOTTIE: That's how I get you.

LEWIS: Why would you joke about cancer?

DOTTIE: Cos no one expects it!

LEWIS: Course they bloody don't!

DOTTIE: So that's how you get them! *(To GABE.)* Got you, didn't I?

She hands him a drink, heads off.

GABRIEL: She has grown into a very… provocative young woman.

LEWIS: D'you know I think Dottie kissed me.

GABRIEL: You think? How could that be a thing you think?

LEWIS: Well I might've… nodded off for a second or two and when I woke up, I could feel – feels like there's lipstick on my mouth?

GABRIEL: Oh yes, there is. Deep red colour. Plum?

LEWIS: And you didn't say anything?

GABRIEL: Well one can't tell these days, it's all cissy boys and she-males, pink hair, girls going round with t-shirts ripped so you can see their… *(He's recalling a specific occasion.)* So I mean it's not all bad but – safety needles through noses? Where's it going to end?

LEWIS: Perhaps it won't.

GABRIEL: That's what worries me. Perhaps it'll just carry on and then –

He takes a drink.

GABRIEL: Cheers.

LEWIS: Your health.

GABRIEL: But still. Swooped in and stole a kiss while you slept, did she? Well that answers the question.

LEWIS: Which question?

GABRIEL: The only question. The question one has to ask about every woman. Does she, or doesn't she. And our Dottie most definitely does.

DOTTIE returns with more glasses.

DOTTIE: Everyone's in here…

VALERIE and ANYA follow her.

VALERIE: Was she very hard work?

ANYA: Hard work for her, or hard work for a normal mum?

VALERIE: Right…

ANYA: Because if you're looking for a normal mum, how d'you find her? You go to her where she lives. Easy. So I did that.

VALERIE: Let me guess: tiresome and loud collection of speed freaks and acid casualties, all twenty years her junior; Mum in the bedroom with the youngest of them.

ANYA: I wish. No it was lights off, curtains drawn, banged at the door for twenty minutes and not a whimper. I went round the corner to a pub to phone, but it didn't even ring. I got a drink, got chatting to the landlord, told my sob story and he says, oh, you're Rainey's girl – she's at the Dorchester.

VALERIE: What was she doing at the Dorchester?

ANYA: She wasn't. She'd gone. With a bill unpaid.

VALERIE: Unlike her…

ANYA: They said they thought she was at a place on the Aldwych – gave me the bill to pass on –

VALERIE: Christ you didn't take it, did you?

ANYA: Well, yeah…

VALERIE: – no no no, if you take things on for her, if *you* take on things that are *her* responsibility –

ANYA: Yes, alright Mum…

They glare at each other.

VALERIE: And when you found her?

8

ANYA: She cried at the sight of me.

VALERIE: *(Beat.)* I think I hate the crying most. Even more than the shagging everything that's got a pulse.

ANYA: Then she said she'd run out of vodka, asked if I'd nip out, get her another bottle. So I did.

ANYA lets that land.

VALERIE: So you're actually aiding and abetting our alcoholic mother now…

ANYA: And once she was three-quarters of the way down the bottle, she became very suggestible. And that enabled me to pour her into a taxi. And it enabled me to haul her onto the train. And she was basically sleeping it off till Carmarthen, so…

VALERIE: You got her here, at least.

LEWIS: She's really here?

ANYA: Outside, flirting with the taxi driver.

LEWIS starts tidying himself up. DOTTIE notices; watches him, amused.

GABRIEL: How on earth did you manage to get a taxi at this time of night?

ANYA: Are you actually asking that?

VALERIE: Rainey gets what she wants.

LEWIS: {What?}

DOTTIE shakes her head.

GABRIEL: I don't think that's always true. Is it.

VALERIE: *(Dismissive rather than wounded.)* Oh right yes, what a bitch I am…

GABRIEL: Now, Valerie, I wasn't / trying to –

VALERIE: What's all this mud?

DOTTIE: I was about to clean it up but then there were coats and drinks and flowers and –

VALERIE: Then perhaps the lesson is don't leave everything till the last minute –

DOTTIE: Well if your bloody boyfriend didn't tramp mud in the house and –

VALERIE: Sorry what?

DOTTIE: Mm?

ANYA: *(To VAL.)* Are you two finally –

DOTTIE leaves, some last minute preparation.

LEWIS: Was that the taxi going?

ANYA: Brace yourselves everyone…

VALERIE: Unless she's gone off with the driver.

ANYA: Oh bloody hell…

VALERIE: *(To LEWIS.)* Now you will actually say something, won't you.

LEWIS: Course.

VALERIE: Yes you say "Course" but will you, when the time comes?

LEWIS: She looks at me, she sees a kid used to run round the yard, cardboard in my daps to fill up the holes. You think she's gonna listen to me?

VALERIE: She looks at me, she sees her daughter. Anyone in the world is more credible than I am – down to and including a cardboard-dapped peasant child.

DOTTIE returns.

DOTTIE: She's coming!

Everyone stands to attention, facing the direction DOTTIE entered from.

No one appears.

ANYA: She bloody has gone off with the taxi driver…

DOTTIE: No, I saw her.

They wait.

VALERIE: *(Calling out.)* Mum?

They wait.

GABRIEL: D'you think we should be – isn't it a bit odd, waiting for her?

VALERIE: What, we should be pretending not to wait for her? Would that be less odd?

GABRIEL: No, I'm just / saying –

ANYA: I think Uncle Gabe's right, it could be a bit pressurising –

RAINEY: Oh you know what she's like – she loves the attention.

And RAINEY is there, behind them at the other side of the room.

VALERIE: Mum!

RAINEY: Daughter.

VALERIE: You're here!

RAINEY: Don't look so shocked, you summoned me didn't you?

VALERIE: We're not shocked, we're just –

GABRIEL: Delighted! We're delighted to see you!

He bear-hugs her –

RAINEY: No that's fine, I wasn't using my ribs for anything.

Plants a kiss on one cheek –

RAINEY: Oh and a kiss.

And another.

RAINEY: Gosh and another.

GABRIEL: We're just…

RAINEY: Delighted, you did say.

GABRIEL: We are! We are!

RAINEY: Would you be so delighted as to go and get my bags? They're in the yard and in the end it will rain.

GABRIEL: But of course.

RAINEY: All this delight, but no one's thought to offer me / [a drink] –

DOTTIE offers her a drink.

DOTTIE: Drink, ma'am?

RAINEY: Thank you ever so much.

VALERIE: Chilled, you'll notice. We do try.

RAINEY: *(To DOTTIE.)* When you say ma'am, it sounds rude. And I don't mean rude in a filthy way. I mean rude as in disrespectful.

DOTTIE: Yes, I know. Good to have you back, ma'am.

GABRIEL: Dottie, my dear –

DOTTIE: ...what?

GABRIEL: Rainey's bags? In the yard? Fetch them in perhaps?

DOTTIE: Well why not.

DOTTIE finishes what she's doing before she goes.

RAINEY: I notice you skulking Lewis. Why are you here?

LEWIS: Friend of the family.

RAINEY: Friend to... which of the family, exactly?

DOTTIE's moving off.

LEWIS: All of you, I like to think.

RAINEY: Greedy.

LEWIS gets up.

LEWIS: Need a hand?

DOTTIE: I never turn one down.

DOTTIE heads off, LEWIS following her.

VALERIE: Lew?

LEWIS: She needs a hand. With the bags.

RAINEY: So: those two then.

VALERIE: Those two what?

RAINEY: Birds of a feather sleep together, as they say.

GABRIEL: Now that's interesting, because Lewis / did mention –

VALERIE: Uncle Gabe, shut up.

GABRIEL: {Sorry...}

ANYA: I don't think they do say that, Mum.

RAINEY: No, but it's what they mean.

She takes a drink. Winces.

RAINEY: You know, there's chilled, and then there's frozen.
And this is –

Meets VALERIE's gaze.

RAINEY: – is you making an effort. Let's be grateful for small
mercies. They tend to be all we get.

She looks around. Puts glass down.

RAINEY: So why am I here?

ANYA: It's late, you should rest / and we can –

RAINEY: Do you think I don't know?

VALERIE: Lew!

RAINEY: What, d'you want a man here to restrain me? He's
welcome to try!

VALERIE: Lewis!

RAINEY: I know what this is. Drag me back on the train, all
the family gathered. This is a, one of those American
things. An intervention.

GABRIEL: What on earth's an intervention?

RAINEY: Where a bunch of busy-bodies get together and take
great pleasure in telling you that you drink too much, well
guess what, I know I drink too much –

VALERIE: It's not an intervention.

ANYA: Why would I buy you vodka, if I was trying to get you
to stop drinking?

RAINEY: I did think you were going a bloody stupid way
about it but –

VALERIE: – what else would you expect of your daughters.

RAINEY: You said that, not me.

ANYA: You *do* drink too much.

RAINEY: I know!

ANYA: You should cut down.

RAINEY: I should cut up!

ANYA: That doesn't even / make sense –

RAINEY: I don't care!

LEWIS arrives back, with bags.

LEWIS: Oh right have you already told her?

VALERIE shakes her head no.

LEWIS: Thought, cos she looks furious, you / must've said –

VALERIE: That's just how she looks.

RAINEY: Told me what?

VALERIE: We're in trouble.

RAINEY smiles.

RAINEY: Oh I know that. {Dot love.}

DOTTIE moves to refill her glass.

VALERIE: We're in trouble, specifically, with money.

RAINEY: Sounds tedious. {Thank you darling}

VALERIE: Bloumfield is in the red every month and it has been, for years.

RAINEY: This all sounds rather like your problem, in fact, not mine –

VALERIE: Lewis, this would be [time for you] –

LEWIS: Mrs Raine –

RAINEY: I am a Mrs, am I. Then where's my mister?

LEWIS struggles.

LEWIS: I don't know what to call you then.

ANYA: Mum!

RAINEY: The staff in general call me ma'am.

LEWIS: I'm not staff.

RAINEY: You look like you should be. Wander out to the kitchen, there's a love, Dottie'll get you a nice bowl of sop, hunk of cheese to go with it.

LEWIS: Alright, yeah, very funny.

RAINEY: What exactly amuses you?

VALERIE: Al. Please.

LEWIS: I've taken a look at your accounts.

RAINEY finds something to do – adjusting with her hair, say – some activity that makes clear she's not paying attention to LEWIS.

LEWIS: It's not that you're in debt; you're in deficit. D'you know the difference?

RAINEY: Should I?

LEWIS snaps.

LEWIS: Course you bloody should!

RAINEY stops fiddling with her hair; looks at him.

RAINEY: Oh this is better, Mr Lewis…

LEWIS: It means every month Bloumfield isn't making enough to cover costs. You're getting deeper in debt, every month.

RAINEY: It seems like my daughter needs to pull her bloody socks up.

LEWIS: But it's you that's legally in control. And whatever she asks, you never answer!

RAINEY: You really are enjoying speaking to me this way, aren't you Mr Lewis.

LEWIS: The bank've had enough. They're foreclosing, they're gonna auction this place.

RAINEY: They can't.

LEWIS: They're gonna sell Bloumfield, and the whole lot of you'll be out.

RAINEY finally takes this on.

RAINEY: Why didn't you say?

VALERIE: I beg your pardon?

RAINEY: Why didn't you tell me, things were –

She cuts herself off. Drinks.

RAINEY: Ah well. I knew you'd screw it up sooner or later. I'm suprised / you've lasted –

VALERIE: Me? Me?

RAINEY: Anya's at university, it is just you. It's a pity I *didn't* leave Dottie in charge, we wouldn't be in this mess –

DOTTIE: We certainly would not.

VALERIE: What about, what about – I wanted us to get organic certification for the bottom fields and you –

RAINEY: I've no idea what she's saying now –

VALERIE: – and I tried to get an answer out of you time after time –

ANYA: She did, Mum.

VALERIE: There was a chap, wanted to rent the fields for his beef herd but it had to be / organic and –

RAINEY: I don't remember any of this.

VALERIE: You don't remember who you slept with last night.

RAINEY: Last night I was on a train, darling. But it's interesting you go straight to my love life. That's where you expect me to be ashamed. I wonder why.

VALERIE: Something to do with my upbringing?

RAINEY: I'll add that to the list of the many, many ways I let down my children.

She holds VALERIE's gaze. VAL says nothing.

RAINEY: Not going to push that one, are we? We dig down and down and finally, we strike decency.

RAINEY drinks.

She looks round the place.

RAINEY: So we're going to lose Bloumfield. *(Beat – Welsh accent.)* There we are then!

LEWIS: There's still a chance, if you pay off the arrears. But, right now. The bank's had enough, we've been fobbing them off for months and –

RAINEY: Then it's simple, someone needs to talk to them, and reassure them it will be paid / in due course.

LEWIS: I've tried that.

RAINEY: Sorry darling I meant a person of substance, a person that a bank manager, might take seriously.

GABRIEL: Oh no, I tried talking to the chap too.

RAINEY: And if I repeat myself now I'm going to sound rude – but it is rather the position you put me in…

LEWIS: We pay off the arrears, and the problem's gone.

RAINEY: But there's no way we can do that –

ANYA: There is a way.

RAINEY: Is there really.

ANYA: But you might not like / it.

VALERIE: She's gonna hate it and sulk like a toddler.

RAINEY: Well if you know there's a way, why the hell / did you drag me back here –

ANYA: Cos you've got to / agree –

VALERIE: It needs your active involvement.

RAINEY: Well that sounds terrifying.

VALERIE: The answer is you sell your flat, and move back home.

RAINEY: I see…

ANYA: I know things are difficult for you here / but –

RAINEY: Oh you know, do you? Tell me what you know.

VALERIE: I have done nothing for myself, I have had nothing for myself just tried to keep this place / going –

RAINEY: Oh dear. Seeing the inheritance slip through your fingers?

VALERIE: Every time you come back, *every time* you catch me out with just how vicious you are.

RAINEY: Thank you darling. It's splendid to see you, too.

She gathers herself.

RAINEY: Of course. Of course. Of course I'd sell the flat to save Bloumfield. You silly little girls.

LEWIS: {*to VALERIE:* What'd I tell you?}

VALERIE: Really?

RAINEY: In a heartbeat.

ANYA: Oh Mum.

ANYA walks up. Takes her hand. Kisses it.

VALERIE: That's –

RAINEY: What, darling?

VALERIE: I feel a bitch now don't I.

RAINEY: That's how you know you're on the right track.

ANYA: We should've known you would. When things really mattered. We should've – thank you.

RAINEY: It's nothing.

VALERIE: No – really.

RAINEY laughs, shrugs.

RAINEY: And I feel a bit... naughty now.

VALERIE senses disaster.

VALERIE: ...why?

RAINEY: I'm afraid darlings the devil is as ever in the detail. What I said was, I would sell the flat. I *would* sell the flat to save Bloumfield. Were I in a position to do so.

ANYA: What d'you mean, Mum?

RAINEY: I had my own little deficit problem, and I never really, I wasn't really, I suppose maintaining the place?

And Tony says you shouldn't hold on to a thing, if you
can't do justice to it –

VALERIE: {Who's Tony?}

ANYA: {Who'd you think?}

RAINEY: – and he's… he's an idiot really but occasionally he'll
pick up the odd thing and repeat it, like some pretty little…
a minah bird or –

VALERIE: What are you going on about?

RAINEY: I sold the flat. Three months ago.

ANYA: You never said!

RAINEY: I probably should have mentioned just I didn't feel it
was any of your damn business.

VALERIE: That's why you were at the Dorchester?

RAINEY: A girl's got to live somewhere! And we thought it'd
be cheaper than owning a whole flat…

VALERIE: And how much have you got left?

RAINEY: Well. Now. Here's the thing. It turns out, it's actually
not cheaper living at a hotel, than / having your own –

VALERIE: / Oh my God…

RAINEY: I know, I am a bit of a handful.

She is wholly unrepentent.

VALERIE: You've wasted all that money?

RAINEY: Yes, and just left you with a house, and an estate, and
land, what an absolute disgrace I am…

VALERIE: A house, and an estate, and land, that we're going to
lose.

RAINEY: I'm sure it's not as bad as all that.

LEWIS: You will lose this place, if you can't pay off the arrears.
That's just how these things work.

RAINEY: I remember your *mam* sending you to our kitchen for
scraps, because your dad drank his wages by Sunday night
– but please. Do go on, about how things work.

She indicates to DOTTIE to top up her glass. DOTTIE does so.

RAINEY: And now I think I'd like to rest. The five hour journey I bore admirably but the last ten minutes... have been murderous. So I shall take myself to bed. Unless someone else would like to take me?

She's looking at LEWIS.

VALERIE: Mum, you're disgusting.

RAINEY: I don't think Alun thinks I'm disgusting. Do you Alun?

Not immediately –

LEWIS: No ma'am.

RAINEY: Oh bugger you then.

RAINEY sweeps off.

ANYA: I can't believe her.

VALERIE: I can.

GABRIEL: I'm sure it's not as bad as all that. You're mother's sharp as a tack, if she thinks there's a way out –

VALERIE: She has no idea, at all.

GABRIEL: Something will come up, you mark my words.

ANYA: D'you really think so?

GABRIEL: It always does.

VALERIE: Uncle Gabe?

GABRIEL: Yes my dear.

VALERIE: Shut up.

GABRIEL: Shutting up...

GABRIEL wanders off.

ANYA: {You alright, unc?}

ANYA follows him. VALERIE turns to LEWIS. Glares at him.

LEWIS: What?

VALERIE: And thanks for all your help.

LEWIS: I did try. And I did tell you she wouldn't listen to me.

VALERIE: You ran off with Dottie, first chance you got.

LEWIS: She needed help with / the bags –

DOTTIE: I was alright with the bags, as it happens. He just come after me.

LEWIS: She's sold the flat. That's not me. That's not my fault. That's your mum.

VALERIE: Thanks for explaining that, I actually heard / myself.

LEWIS: So what the hell you laying into me for?

She doesn't answer.

DOTTIE: Come after me again if you like, Al.

DOTTIE goes.

VALERIE: The cheek of that girl.

LEWIS: …well yeah.

VALERIE: D'you like her?

LEWIS: Like her how?

VALERIE looks at him.

LEWIS: You mean like her like her? Good God no.

VALERIE: She's very attractive.

LEWIS: Not my type.

VALERIE: I would've said she was.

LEWIS: Peasant stock, you mean?

VALERIE: Salt of the earth. Very earthy. Very salty.

LEWIS: Joking aside though –

VALERIE: {oh, we were *joking*, were we…}

LEWIS: – I think Dottie kissed me.

VALERIE: How can you *think* she kissed you? Either she did / or she –

LEWIS: I was resting my eyes a sec on the settee and then she was standing over me – and I could feel lipstick, on my lips.

VALERIE: So that is lipstick on your mouth, I did wonder.

LEWIS: Is it still on there? Why didn't you say.

VALERIE: I just thought you were being... weird.

LEWIS: So she kissed me. When I was asleep.

VALERIE: No she didn't...

LEWIS: Well there was no one else about.

VALERIE: My mum's after you, my housekeeper's after you...

LEWIS: Why no mun, your mum was just teasing.

VALERIE: And so was Dottie.

VAL moves.

VALERIE: She didn't kiss you. She doesn't wear make-up at work. Puts it on if she's going straight out. But never when she's working.

LEWIS: How d'you know that?

VALERIE: Cos I can see it?

VALERIE calls off.

VALERIE: Dot!

DOT appears.

DOTTIE: You shout?

VALERIE: Need you a second.

DOTTIE: 'Salright, I wasn't in the middle of anything...

She's ostentatiously drying her hands with a tea towel.

VALERIE: You don't wear make-up when you come to work, do you?

DOTTIE: No. Put it on to go home but –

VALERIE: You see?

DOTTIE: – it doesn't do to make your boss look dowdy, so never at work...

VALERIE: That's very considerate of you.

DOTTIE: Well I try. Finished with me now?

VALERIE: God yes.

DOTTIE leaves them.

VALERIE and LEWIS look at each other.

LEWIS: Cheeky little mare!

VALERIE: Then perhaps don't fall asleep with your feet up on my sofa.

She's brushing dirt from the sofa cover. Stops.

Looks around the place.

VALERIE: We're going to lose it all.

LEWIS: I can try talking to the bank again…

VALERIE: And tell them what?

She looks round her.

VALERIE: All these years I've worked and –

LEWIS: If I had the money to buy the place for you, I would, but –

VALERIE: Do you?

LEWIS: What?

VALERIE: Have the money to buy the place?

LEWIS: No, that's what I'm saying. But if I did…

VALERIE: Well that's a really useful thing to say, that really helps, thank you.

LEWIS is at a loss.

Pours a glass of wine. Gives it to her.

VALERIE: Slightly more use.

She drinks.

VALERIE: Your health.

Drinks again.

VALERIE: Bollocks bollocks bollocks.

LEWIS steps towards her.

Steps again. Puts down his glass.

Is about to move closer –

VALERIE: Just, leave me be for a bit. Will you.

LEWIS goes.

VALERIE stands.

Sound grows. The sounds of the place. Clock, room tone. Sounds of outside. The garden, the woods, the stream –

– and wave after wave after wave crashing against the shore.

It all snaps away.

A wooden toy truck rolls on. Stops not far from VALERIE.

VALERIE is petrified. Doesn't move.

Then looks down at it. Looks away.

Then walks over to it, picks it up.

VALERIE: I know. I'm sorry.

She speaks not to herself; but out, to the room.

She leans down, gently rolls the truck back in the direction it came.

She stands.

Walks back to where she was.

Suddenly becomes aware LEWIS is back, just at the edge of the space.

She looks at him: what?

LEWIS: I've got an idea. I wouldn't've thought you're gonna like it.

TWO

The next morning.

GABRIEL wanders into the room.

GABRIEL: Hello?

No response.

Turns to look at books on a shelf. Then suddenly –

GABRIEL: Who's there?

GABE's looking to one side of stage. DOTTIE enters from the other, not stopping.

DOTTIE: Morning.

GABRIEL: Well, quite.

DOTTIE keeps moving.

GABRIEL: Coffee'd be a treat.

DOTTIE: Yeah, I need a couple to get myself [going] –

She cuts herself off.

DOTTIE: You want me, to make you a coffee?

GABRIEL: A little milk, and two / sugar –

DOTTIE: One thing at a time, keep your hair on –

She's heading off.

GABRIEL wanders back to the bookshelf.

Rubs dust off the top of the books.

Is intrigued by a title. Pulls the book out

Opens it. Begins to read.

Is very quickly appalled by what he reads.

DOTTIE enters with the jug from a filter machine, a cup, sugar and milk, all on a tray.

GABE quickly puts the book back in the shelf.

DOTTIE: You alright?

25

GABRIEL: Yes just… admiring the shelf.

DOTTIE laughs at him.

DOTTIE: Why?

GABRIEL: It's wonderful.

DOTTIE: Worth something?

GABRIEL: I'd think so.

DOTTIE's been waiting for GABE to come and get his coffee. He's clearly not going to. So – as they speak – she pours a cup, adds milk and sugar, gives it a stir, clatters down the spoon.

GABRIEL: But it's the – the worksmanship. The skill. The *care.*

DOTTIE: So what coupla hundred?

GABRIEL: Much more.

DOTTIE: Really?

She hands him the coffee.

GABRIEL: You are a darling.

He takes a sip. Not good.

GABRIEL: Mm. Okay.

DOTTIE: So… thousand maybe?

GABRIEL: My grand-father commissioned this. And the chap was weeks making it. Sawing, planing, sanding, the detail here – you see?

He's pointing to a little flourish on the shelf.

DOTTIE: Catches the dust a bugger there.

GABRIEL: Yes it does. Possibly someone should clean it.

DOTTIE: Yeah you'd think.

GABRIEL: And no one bothers these days. It's your chipboard rubbish. Glued together and comes apart in your hands.

DOTTIE: 'Swhat people can afford.

GABRIEL: But it's a false economy – I've just said, just now, it comes apart in your – but this. This was made when I was a boy. And it's still in great shape.

DOTTIE: Yeah, it's grand. If you can afford it.

GABRIEL: But such things *were* affordable. In those days it wasn't about turning a profit. The man that made this – the craftsman – he did the job, to do the job.

DOTTIE: What he do to eat then?

GABRIEL: Obviously he was paid for his labour, I'm saying – he worked to make a beautiful thing. And his reward was not so much in his wage packet, it was the knowledge that he had made, this beautiful thing –

DOTTIE: And Christmas they'd let him up the manor for a tot of sherry and maybe, he'd catch a glimpse of it on his way out.

GABRIEL: And the knowledge that it would last, long after him –

DOTTIE: He's dead is he, bloke that made it?

GABRIEL: Well I mean –

GABRIEL realises he has no idea.

GABRIEL: I don't know. I presume so, but –

Gathers himself.

GABRIEL: I'm saying, that craftsman worked, late into the night, long beyond the point he was making money out of it, to make something functional and beautiful. And we don't do that any more. And we're the worse for it.

DOTTIE: Craftsman? He was a waste of space.

GABRIEL: I beg your pardon?

DOTTIE: Might as well be down the pub drinking his wages as in his workshop, slaving over something he's not getting paid for. His kids are going hungry either way.

GABRIEL: Well if everyone thought the way you do –

DOTTIE: Everyone does.

GABRIEL: I don't think / they do –

DOTTIE: *(Over him.)* Read a paper, mun.

He stares at her.

DOTTIE: What?

He drains his cup.

GABRIEL: Couldn't get me a top up, could you?

She takes his cup, goes back to the table. He watches her walk away.

GABRIEL: {Goodness me...}

She stops. Looks at him.

He's all innocence.

GABRIEL: Mmm?

And CERI is there.

CERI: I feel... as if I've walked in on something. Have I?

GABRIEL: Ah. Now. Now...

GABRIEL's staring meaningfully at CERI.

GABRIEL: I'm sorry, I can't quite place you.

CERI: No, I get that a lot.

He turns to DOTTIE. Takes her in.

CERI: And how are you?

She's deciding whether to find him obnoxious or charming.

Decides. Both.

DOTTIE: Yes, alright, hello.

CERI: I heard a whisper Rainey's back.

DOTTIE: She is, yeah.

CERI: Is she alright?

GABRIEL: She's on grand form, thank you – but, sorry, I'm still / not sure –

DOTTIE: Course she's not alright.

CERI: She's not – dying or anything?

GABRIEL: Well aren't we all?

DOTTIE: I think Rainey's going at it bit harder than most of us.

CERI: For obvious reasons.

GABRIEL: Sorry – who *are* you?

CERI: I'm Ceri. Friend of the family.

GABRIEL: I'm 'of the family', I've no idea who you are.

DOTTIE: He used to help out Anya, with her maths and –

CERI: More her English, and history, and – but yes maths too.

DOTTIE: So she'd get into university.

CERI: So she'd comprehend the world, and the forces that shape it. But yeah I got the girl into uni, for my sins.

ANYA enters.

ANYA: *(As she's entering.)* Did I hear –

She comes to a complete stop when she claps eyes on CERI.

ANYA: – oh.

They stare at one another. Both struck by one another – seeing one another as adults, rather than as tutor and student. DOTTIE sees it happen.

DOTTIE: Oh yeah Anya's back too.

CERI: Mmm?

DOTTIE: Oh, don't mind me.

Then ANYA packs it away.

ANYA: How are you?

CERI: Really really fantastic, now.

GABRIEL: So you two know each other?

ANYA: Ceri was my tutor, when I was doing A-levels.

DOTTIE: I said that to you, two minutes ago.

GABRIEL: You can't expect me to remember every little thing...

CERI: What brings you home?

ANYA: The estate is bankrupt and we're going to lose everything.

GABRIEL: Actually –

CERI: Brilliant.

ANYA: I'm sorry?

29

CERI: You should lose it.

GABRIEL: – the estate is fine. The estate is making money. It's the house. Bloumfield itself. Costs the earth to keep it going. Listed building and all that.

ANYA: Why should we?

CERI: Well that's easy then!

GABRIEL: Is it? Do tell.

CERI: Knock the house down. Build something better.

GABRIEL: Ah I see, ah very good.

CERI: Make something new and modern, that doesn't cost the earth to keep going.

GABRIEL: But of course! Why didn't we think?

CERI: Problem solved!

ANYA: I would rather miss the place though. What with, having grown up here. All my memories. All our family. Going back generations.

CERI: But it sounds like you can't afford any of those things, can you?

ANYA: Oh, well in that case...

GABRIEL: Darling child, something will come up.

CERI: Yeah, probably. It usually does. For people like you.

GABRIEL notices something out the window.

ANYA: What d'you mean, people like us?

GABRIEL: Did you see that – my God...

GABRIEL shoots off.

CERI: Just – rich people. Things have a way of working out for you. *(Beat.)* I wonder if it's something to do with all your money?

ANYA: You know I don't remember you being such an arse, when you tutored me.

CERI: You were very young, so I kept it under wraps. How's university?

ANYA: Great thanks.

CERI: How's the law?

ANYA: I switched.

CERI: Good, what to?

ANYA: History and fine art.

CERI: You're only wasting half your time then.

ANYA: I beg your pardon?

CERI: History. History's worth knowing. Fine art though...

ANYA: And what are you doing?

CERI: All sorts of things.

ANYA: To earn a living.

CERI: Which of course defines what I am. I teach adults who can't read, to read.

ANYA: Okay. *(Beat.)* That's really good.

CERI: Yes it is. I'm really good for doing that.

ANYA: You might do a really good thing for a living, you can still actually be an arsehole.

CERI: Fine art – any art that needs explaining so you can get it – is not art. It's just conspicuous consumption. Which means –

ANYA: It's wasting money on something useless just to show off you've got money to waste. So all art is nonsense then.

CERI: No; there are things that affect or engage the ordinary man – music say – they are art and –

ANYA: Your dad used to love Status Quo.

CERI: Yes he did.

ANYA: So Status Quo are art, and...

CERI: Status Quo are vile, but if you'd said Roxy Music...

ANYA: So Status Quo are art, but... the paintings of Mark Rothko are not, because your dad says so.

CERI: Yes.

ANYA: You're gonna stand by that, are you?

CERI doesn't answer immediately.

ANYA: D'you know who Mark Rothko is?

CERI: Does big splashy paintings like a five year old. What are they actually of?

ANYA: Which ones have you seen?

CERI: Like ninety-nine per cent of humanity, none at all. And / I'm fine –

ANYA: Because I saw one at MoMA in New York and it was a painting of how my heart broke one night when I was a very little girl.

She stares at him.

CERI: Which is the kind of thing you get to say, when you've got a degree in fine art. To my dad it's a big painting like a five year old would do. Only he wouldn't dare say that. Cos people like you would laugh at him.

ANYA: And what would you say? If you weren't afraid of me laughing at you.

CERI: D'you know, your dressing gown's come right open?

ANYA doesn't panic, holds his gaze, does nothing to check on her gown.

ANYA: No it hasn't. You know how I know that?

She begins slowly walking towards him.

ANYA: Because under this gown, I am wearing absolutely nothing. Not a stitch. And if my gown had come open, I would feel the breeze, on all my bare skin. And you would not be staring quite so unwaveringly into my eyes.

CERI: Maybe I'm being a gentlemen.

ANYA: I know a few of those. You are not one.

CERI: I think, you and me should probably go for a drink.

ANYA: I'm sure that'd be great fun. Not sure what my partner would think about it.

CERI: Boyfriend back in uni? Let me guess – sporty type. Rugby / lad –

ANYA: No boyfriend, back in uni.

CERI: Then – bloody hell.

ANYA: That smile is a picture...

CERI: We are definitely going for a drink.

ANYA: Cos a girlfriend doesn't count?

CERI: If you haven't got a boyfriend, that leaves you with a... vacancy.

ANYA: She fills all my vacancies, thank you.

CERI: Oh good God...

GABRIEL charges in.

GABRIEL: Well I couldn't find the little sods.

CERI: I think I need to sit down...

ANYA: If you can. *(To GABRIEL.)* Find who, Uncle?

GABRIEL: Boys in the orchard, scrumping apples.

ANYA: I didn't see any boys?

GABRIEL: A boy, at least.

VALERIE and LEWIS enter, dressed for a decent walk.

LEWIS: I'm right though aren't I. It's the only place.

ANYA: Long way to walk for a few apples.

VALERIE: *(To LEWIS.)* I suppose you are, yes. Ceri, how are you?

GABRIEL: Well no doubt they have bicycles.

CERI: Chastened. Troubled. But in a good way.

VALERIE has no time for this.

VALERIE: *(To LEWIS.)* You know Ceri?

LEWIS: I know of him.

GABRIEL: *(To VAL and LEWIS.)* Did you see them?

VALERIE: *(To GABRIEL.)* See who?

GABRIEL: Boys scrumping apples.

ANYA: You said *a* boy.

GABRIEL: One confirmed sighting. I suspect there was a gang.

VALERIE: In the orchard? D'you get a look at him?

GABRIEL: He was – you know, a boy. Familiar looking but – aren't they all.

Not instantly, but VAL retreats from the conversation; goes to a corner to take off her coat, scarf, and sit down quietly.

GABRIEL: *(To CERI.)* It's the principle of the thing!

CERI: Hanging's too good for them!

GABRIEL: *(To VAL.)* You should get a keeper up here.

VALERIE doesn't answer.

GABRIEL: I said you should get a keeper up here. They get the idea they can steal and get away with it, you'll have a plague of them. They'll strip the orchard. Valerie!

VALERIE: We've got plenty of fruit. More than we can sell.

GABRIEL: No wonder the place is going to ruin, if that's your attitude…

LEWIS: So we'd have a gamekeeper, to protect the fruit.

GABRIEL: I'm not saying shoot them, I'm saying scare them off!

LEWIS: Cost more to pay a gamekeeper, than you'd lose in kids scrumping apples.

GABRIEL: Yes alright, not a gamekeeper then –

LEWIS: Someone cheaper.

GABRIEL: Well yes.

LEWIS: A young lad maybe, just starting out.

GABRIEL: Yes, exactly.

LEWIS: He'll still want paying something.

GABRIEL: But not much.

LEWIS: And this place is losing money already –

GABRIEL: Well then –

LEWIS: Tell you what. Val says orchard gives more fruit than she can sell. So you could give this lad, the spare fruit.

GABRIEL: You see? These things just take a little thinking about, not instant sniping...

LEWIS: So your plan is, stop lads coming and taking the fruit – by getting a lad, and giving him the fruit.

GABRIEL: Oh yes very clever. Alright, I like you, you can stay.

LEWIS: I think I am.

GABRIEL: Now. I need breakfast, but *(Finds ANYA.)* be of good cheer. All will be well, and all will be well, and all manner of thing will be well.

VALERIE: Up early as usual.

ANYA: What d'you mean, it's nearly – oh yeah, lazy student, really funny.

VALERIE: Going to get dressed at any point?

ANYA: No, I thought I'd parade myself all day.

VALERIE: Why not. You won't have those looks forever.

ANYA: *(Leaving.)* Yes, I'll just have my intelligence and education to fall back on, how will I manage.

GABRIEL: You could marry her off, have you thought of that?

VALERIE: Many, many times...

CERI: Although nowadays marrying a daughter off to a wealthy young lord isn't quite the done thing.

GABRIEL: Were you attempting an impression of me then? It was dreadful if you were.

CERI: Not so much you specifically, more a generic, you know, your type –

GABRIEL: Fair enough then. *(To VALERIE.)* Obviously I don't mean a forced thing but – get her out and about, introduce her to a few eligible and attractive young men of means and... let nature take its course. Like finds like, always.

CERI: So she's bound to end up with a posh boy.

GABRIEL: In the end, of course. No doubt a few tumbles in the hay with some rough and ready types along the way...

CERI: Because I thought she was a lesbian.

GABRIEL: Is she really?

VALERIE: No, she's not.

GABRIEL: Because at one time almost everybody was.

VALERIE: She's just dabbling.

GABRIEL: Is that what they call it nowadays...

CERI: Couldn't cope with an actual lesbian in the family, Val?

RAINEY enters.

RAINEY: Christ it's all real.

VALERIE: Where did you sleep, Mum?

RAINEY: Guest room, attic.

VALERIE: But we didn't – we put fresh sheets on your bed –

RAINEY: Then that was a waste of time. Why isn't there coffee? DOTTIE!

CERI: Elizabeth, I heard you were back.

RAINEY: Did you, well, hello.

RAINEY likes the look of him but can't place him.

CERI: It's / Ceri, I was –

RAINEY: Oh it's Ceri, hello!

She opens her arms, and they hug.

RAINEY: Were you always this delicious or have you improved with age?

CERI: I was much better than this, years ago.

RAINEY: What the hell was I thinking letting you near my daughter! Well I know what *I* was thinking...

CERI: How is London?

RAINEY: Still there, I presume. I don't see much of it. Live very quietly you know, keep myself to myself.

GABRIEL: Now you're up Rainey I was just saying, you've got a bit of a scrumping problem, you need to get a lad or –

LEWIS: *(To VAL.)* {I *just* explained to him –}

VALERIE shrugs in answer to LEWIS as GABRIEL continues.

GABRIEL: – a few lads actually to keep an eye / on the orchard –

DOTTIE arrives, talks over GABRIEL.

DOTTIE: Sorry did you scream?

RAINEY: Why've you left me with these people?

DOTTIE: Your family?

RAINEY: So you know what you've done. The full enormity, of your / crime.

DOTTIE: You want coffee or booze?

RAINEY: What d'you think I'm going to say, if you / ask me

DOTTIE: The coffee is already on.

RAINEY: *(Beat.)* Fair enough, coffee then.

DOTTIE heads off to get the coffee.

RAINEY: We don't pay her anything like enough.

VALERIE: Why, how much do we pay her?

RAINEY: It was a flippant / comment –

VALERIE: I send you the accounts every month, I had no idea you actually read them…

RAINEY: I feel for whatever man you eventually manage to clamp your legs around, I really do.

LEWIS: We went for a walk, Mrs Raine.

She has no idea how to take this.

RAINEY: Well that's… lovely, and what else have you done with the morning?

DOTTIE enters with coffee. She's coming straight to RAINEY but RAINEY beckons her anyway.

RAINEY: Painted a little picture? Wandered down the crossing to see a train go past?

VALERIE: We've got a plan to save Bloumfield.

RAINEY takes the coffee, takes a gulp.

RAINEY: That's unreasonably hot.

DOTTIE: I boiled the water.

DOTTIE heads off, and comes on with more cups, milk, the pot from a filter coffee maker, and gets coffee for everyone.

VALERIE: Mum?

RAINEY turns to her.

RAINEY: You said it couldn't be saved.

LEWIS: One thing you learn in business, always have a plan B.

RAINEY: ...I'm sorry come again?

LEWIS: Have a plan B. In case plan A doesn't come off.

RAINEY: Little Alun Lewis. You stand here and say these darling grown-up things and – I remember your dad belting you one morning in the burgage for – existing really and you, bawling your eyes out, and I scooped you up. Put you on my knees. Hugged you to my breasts. You liked that.

VALERIE: Mum.

LEWIS: Listen you. I can save this place. And I bloody will, if you'll let me. But I got a crap load of other things I could be doing this morning so if you don't wanna know say now and I'll be off.

DOTTIE stops what she's doing. Everyone waiting for RAINEY's explosion.

But RAINEY doesn't respond.

LEWIS: Well?

RAINEY: Well this is me listening. Mr Lewis.

DOTTIE: {Bloody hell...}

LEWIS: Alright then.

LEWIS realises all eyes are on him. A little unnerved by it. He gathers himself.

LEWIS: You know the last couple years thanks to Mrs Thatcher, people can buy their council houses?

RAINEY: If you say so.

ANYA: It has been quite big news.

RAINEY: Perhaps at university, darling.

LEWIS: So people get to buy their houses at what – half the price they're worth. Massive bargain. Everyone who can, is snapping them up. And you drive round the estates, you can tell straight off which house have been bought. You know how?

RAINEY: It is a little while since I drove round a council estate, I'll confess.

LEWIS: They're the ones've been done up. New doors, uPVC windows. Pebble dash on the walls. People will spend money on a house that's really theirs. But here's the thing. You can do your ex-council house up all you like, but there's one thing you can't change. You're still living on a scummy council estate. And no amount of pebble dash is gonna change that.

RAINEY: I know this isn't really my world, but –

VALERIE: Give him a sec, Mum.

LEWIS: All these people have been handed a house, at half price. And they can sell that house, at full price. And buy another house. A better house. That isn't, on a scummy council estate.

DOTTIE: I wish you'd stop saying that...

LEWIS: *(To DOTTIE.)* Sorry love, no offence. *(To RAINEY.)* So I'm gonna build houses for them.

RAINEY: Well, good luck with that.

LEWIS: And I'm gonna clean up, aren't I. I buy a field – farmer's field, it's worth nothing, grand if you're lucky, cos farming makes nothing. But that same field. I can build a couple dozen houses on it, sell each one for – twenty, maybe thirty thousand quid. So you're looking at – half a million quid. For a field.

GABRIEL: Bloody hell.

LEWIS: Oh yeah. And say somebody was to sell me a field – well I'd give to them better than farm prices.

GABRIEL: How much, exactly?

LEWIS: Well you know that's to be negotiated. But fifty thou, hundred…

GABRIEL: Well I mean we'll sell. Of course we will, for a hundred thousand –

VALERIE: It's not as simple / as that –

RAINEY: Oh – there's a catch. Quelle surprise.

LEWIS: The catch is – you haven't got a field I could build on. By the house it's too much of a slope, down to the sea it floods, it's boggy, no services.

RAINEY: So then…?

VALERIE: So then there is one place, that's ideal.

LEWIS: The orchards. It's flat, natural drainage. Road right by it.

ANYA: But – the orchards?

LEWIS: Half a dozen men with chainsaws, drott to dig out the stumps. Gone in a week.

ANYA's appalled.

VALERIE: I know, I know: but if it saves everything else…

RAINEY: And we'd have – a new little village, right on our doorstep. Overnight.

LEWIS: Not overnight, you'd be looking eighteen, twenty-four months at least for the building / work –

VALERIE: That much money would turn our finances around. We'd have plenty left to invest, to make this place work as a farm. Bloumfield would be safe, forever.

LEWIS: It'll work, Mrs Raine. I swear to God. I can do this.

RAINEY: You sound very confident –

LEWIS: Because I am.

RAINEY: – I was going to say, for a ditch-digger's son.

RAINEY pauses. Fiddles with something – an ornament.

CERI: And what about everybody else?

LEWIS: Everybody else who?

VALERIE: Mum?

CERI: Everybody who can't afford to buy a house. They can't rent one from the council, cos Maggie Thatcher sold them off.

LEWIS: Everyone'll be able to afford a house.

CERI: What's she gonna do, exterminate all the poor people?

ANYA: Not exterminate, surely. Just sterilise.

LEWIS smiles.

LEWIS: Maggie Thatcher's made a market for houses. And cos of that, people like me are building houses. So there are gonna be more houses than there used to be. And more houses, means houses get cheaper. Everybody'll be able to afford one. Basic supply and demand.

VALERIE: Mum, what do you think?

RAINEY: Well, you've worked out all the details.

LEWIS: So do we go ahead?

She doesn't answer.

LEWIS: Like I said, I got loads of other things / I could be –

VALERIE puts a hand on his arm, stopping him.

VALERIE: What do you say, Anya?

ANYA: Well I mean I don't – the orchards, they've just always been there.

LEWIS: They haven't. Her dad planted them.

ANYA: Thank you, I know that, I mean – in my life, when I
was little girl –

She turns to VALERIE.

ANYA: – we'd spend days, building dens in the trees, and dams
in the streams and – and with Joseph.

The name lands with everyone in the room.

RAINEY and ANYA looking at each other.

ANYA: But if this it what it takes, to save Bloumfield. We lose
the orchards, but we save everything else.

LEWIS: I guarantee we will.

ANYA: Then yes.

RAINEY: How long did it take you to come up with this little
plan, eh?

LEWIS: I think quick. And like I said: plan B.

RAINEY: And isn't it amazing how your quick thinking leads
right to ripping down those orchards.

LEWIS: It'll work.

RAINEY: I bet. *(To her daughters.)* Did he tell you?

VALERIE: So Mum. Anya's for it.

RAINEY: {You're not even interested...}

VALERIE: And I am. And –

RAINEY: Everyone's decided then. We're going to have
hundreds of happy families – the very cream of the county's
council tenants – slap bang right up against us, forever.

DOTTIE stops what she's doing.

LEWIS: It's this, or lose everything – the house, / the land –

A dangerous look from VALERIE.

LEWIS: What?

VALERIE: Just give her, a moment.

RAINEY: It's still my choice, isn't it. Legally.

GABRIEL: Of course.

RAINEY: Then I say no.

VALERIE stares at her.

RAINEY: Sorry darling what was that?

VALERIE stalks off. LEWIS follows her.

DOTTIE: Switching to booze now?

RAINEY: Sun's past the yardarm. Somewhere.

DOTTIE hands her a drink, rather roughly, spilling some.

RAINEY: {Share it with the carpet, why not...}

DOTTIE begins dusting and polishing things furiously.

ANYA: I can't believe you'd do this.

RAINEY: Well: you're very young.

GABRIEL: *(To ANYA.)* Something will turn up. Something always does.

CERI: Something always has. Times change, Uncle.

ANYA leaves, upset.

CERI: Oh, balls…

CERI goes after her.

GABRIEL: Do you remember great-aunt Ninnie?

RAINEY: Gabriel –

GABRIEL: Yes?

RAINEY: Shut up.

He wanders away.

DOTTIE's polishing something. Very fiercely.

RAINEY: You're going to wear through that table.

DOTTIE: Bit of what they call a stubborn stain.

RAINEY: Dottie!

DOTTIE throws down the cloth.

DOTTIE: I live on a council estate.

RAINEY: Really? You haven't got the smell.

DOTTIE: I never thought you were a snob.

RAINEY: Oh don't be ridiculous, I'm a *massive* snob.

DOTTIE stares her down.

And RAINEY crumbles.

RAINEY: I don't mean you, do I.

DOTTIE: You don't want people from estates living by you. I'm from an estate. You bloody / do mean –

RAINEY: It's not anyone in particular, it's just – as a group, when there / are dozens of them –

DOTTIE: So me on my own's fine, but me and the kids...

RAINEY: Have you got dozens of kids?

RAINEY's very much joking. DOTTIE stares at her: turns away. Picks up her.

DOTTIE: Was there anything else you wanted, ma'am?

RAINEY: Oh come on...

DOTTIE: Because if there's nothing else, I do have duties / around the house –

RAINEY: Now I don't deserve that.

DOTTIE: I'll take my leave then, ma'am.

DOTTIE curtseys.

RAINEY: You're being a bloody child, and I won't pander to it.

DOTTIE sweeps off.

RAINEY: Dottie!

She turns.

DOTTIE: And what will happen to me?

RAINEY doesn't get it.

DOTTIE: If this place is sold. What about me?

RAINEY: You? Of all of us, you're the one I'm worried about least. You can look after yourself.

DOTTIE: Well I have to.

RAINEY shifts.

RAINEY: D'you remember your mum always – would sit, about this time with – she'd have tea, in a bowl, and bread it in – what did they call that?

DOTTIE: Sop.

RAINEY: Yes, her big bowl of sop and then these fistfuls of Cheddar. She'd feed me little tidbits of cheese, like I was a bird.

They look at each other.

RAINEY: I'd love a few big lumps of cheese. To really chew at, you know?

DOTTIE: We have Cheddar in the pantry. You want the sop too?

RAINEY: Christ no, I hate peasant food.

It's a test: is the spat really repaired?

DOTTIE: Stuck-up cow.

RAINEY: And proud of it!

DOTTIE's moving off.

DOTTIE: Crackers?

RAINEY: Not according to my shrink!

DOTTIE: With the cheese?

RAINEY: No, thank you, but – do we have some lovely ripe grapes?

DOTTIE: I believe we do.

RAINEY: And a glass of a nice robust red to go with them.

DOTTIE: But of course.

DOTTIE's nearly gone.

RAINEY: You know what? Actually forget the cheese.

DOTTIE: Still want grapes?

RAINEY: No point without the Cheddar.

DOTTIE: So just the glass of red.

RAINEY: You *are* a darling, thanks a million.

As DOTTIE's leaving –

RAINEY: Just don't be stingy with it.

From elsewhere, VALERIE enters.

RAINEY doesn't see her immediately; then does. Slumps.

RAINEY: Oh, God…

VALERIE: I haven't come to have a go, so spare me the look.

RAINEY: Which is having a go, isn't it. It obviously is.

VALERIE: D'you think other mothers behave like this?

RAINEY: I don't think I… know any other mothers. Certainly none that would bring up the fact in conversation.

DOTTIE enters with wine, cheese and grapes.

RAINEY: I said not the cheese!

DOTTIE's putting things down.

RAINEY: I get no respect.

DOTTIE: Think you deserve any?

RAINEY looks up at DOTTIE. DOTTIE carries on putting things down.

RAINEY grabs her hand, clutches it.

DOTTIE doesn't react, just stays with it.

RAINEY lets go.

VALERIE watching all this.

DOTTIE heads off.

RAINEY: *(The food.)* Don't leave it, I'll only pick.

DOTTIE: That's the idea.

RAINEY stares at the food, annoyed.

Then gets up.

RAINEY: You like cheese don't you darling?

VALERIE: Not / really

RAINEY: Then it can't do any harm if I put it… next to you.

RAINEY leaves the cheese near VALERIE, retreats to her chair.

Takes a big gulp of wine.

RAINEY: Oh that is... absolutely / sublime –

VALERIE: Can I have some?

The wine.

RAINEY: Best not, you know how you get. Tuck in to that lovely cheese!

VALERIE has a nibble.

RAINEY: Excellent. A few curves would help you no end.

VALERIE: Help me how?

RAINEY: With your life.

VALERIE stares at her.

RAINEY: Yes, give me the glare. You look like a furious mouse!

VALERIE puts down the cheese.

VALERIE: It's not worth / even trying –

RAINEY: No, not many mothers are like me. Because not many mothers, are like me.

VALERIE: I know that...

RAINEY: You know, but I think you forget. I don't forget.

VALERIE: Yes alright.

VALERIE's given way.

RAINEY: Look at us! We're having wine and cheese. Like proper people!

They sit together.

RAINEY: Isn't that lovely? A comfortable silence. Why not try that out every now and again. Just... being... quiet –

VALERIE: It has not been –

RAINEY: Oh God.

VALERIE: – it has not been nothing, keeping this place going.

RAINEY: You have mentioned.

She takes a drink.

RAINEY: And I'm very grateful

It feels like a genuine admission.

VALERIE: And I don't know why I bothered.

RAINEY: No one knows why you bothered. *(Takes a drink.)* Entirely baffling.

It sounds like RAINEY is being typically flip; but VALERIE feels like she might have heard a truth.

VALERIE: Because it was the thing to do. To carry on. Cos I thought you'd come back.

RAINEY: Did you?

VALERIE: Yes of course. At first, yeah. I thought you'd get it out of your system –

RAINEY: {– oh –}

VALERIE: – and then you'd – [come back]. But then – no after *years* I knew, you weren't coming back.

RAINEY: Brave little Val, struggling to keep the place afloat when everyone else has abandoned ship. Very noble.

VALERIE: I didn't think it would be – I mean I hate it. Rattling around the place with just Dottie. The house being empty it feels wrong. Although I mean it's not empty.

RAINEY looks at her.

VALERIE: Is it.

RAINEY looks away.

VALERIE: I was with this foster family in Milford before you adopted me.

RAINEY: I do know yes.

VALERIE: Horrible but I loved the woman, Nellie. She never hit me, and she kicked out her husband when he did. The house was damp, I remember one room they just couldn't go in and the black mould on my bedroom ceiling. My throat would catch in the morning from breathing it. And I cried when they took from Nellie and she cried too. They brought me here, and you barely looked at me twice. I walked round the place. All the rooms. Ending up sitting in the kitchen legs swinging under the table and the cook – Dottie's mum it was – gave me a slice of bread and butter with sugar on it and I put it away three big mouthfuls. And the clock, ticking tocking. The fire piled with logs. That bloody bookshelf. And the gardens. The fields. The orchards. The streams right down to the sea. All of it. Bloody all of it. And you said, so would you like to come and live with us. And I said yes please. And you offered me your hand said, that's what we'll do then. And I shook your hand. I went back home. Packed up my things. Nellie bawling her eyes out. Arms stretched out to hug me. And I offered her my hand.

She pauses.

VALERIE: I thought if I could fill the place up again. If it was full with a family. If you could come back and not be... the kind of mother you are. If you could come back and be grandma –

RAINEY: You think I'm ready for grandma?

VALERIE: Yes. If you want it.

RAINEY: I don't want it.

VALERIE: If it happened anyway.

RAINEY: You and who is this?

VALERIE: Me and Lew.

RAINEY: *Lewis?* And you?

VALERIE: We're a good team.

RAINEY: I mean possibly but – what do I know about these things.

VALERIE: Oh great.

RAINEY: Just / ignore me –

VALERIE: I typically have to.

She wants to give up; won't.

VALERIE: I kept thinking of summer. How summers might be. After the harvest playing great games of rounders with the sun going down, and tops exploding out of bottles of homebrew. A bonfire the size of a house Guy Fawkes night. Christmas dinners with more people round the table than it can fit; and kids ripping into presents, and a tree bent up against the ceiling. And people wandering up singing carols New Year's morning, hungover to buggery but wanting another little tot of sherry to keep the cold off. And me rushed off my bloody feet keeping it all going. But never minding. Never once. And you – you're wrapped in a blanket. Drink in your hand.

RAINEY: As ever.

VALERIE: As ever. And your grand-kids bloody adoring you. And you loving them back. Whether you want to or not.

RAINEY looks at her.

VALERIE: He wouldn't mind.

RAINEY looks away, shrugs.

VALERIE: I asked him.

RAINEY looks back at her. VALERIE holds her gaze.

She mouths something to RAINEY.

VALERIE: I know. I know.

RAINEY puts down her drink.

RAINEY: Oh God.

VALERIE: That this place could be full of light and warmth and noise again.

RAINEY: Well I wish you all the best. You and Lewis.

VALERIE: But it needs you.

RAINEY: Nothing is more likely to ruin things, than me.

VALERIE: I've done nothing for myself. Had nothing for myself. Just kept this place going, for you. So the story doesn't end with a… with a beach. Or a car crash. So it goes on after all that. So it ends with light and warmth and noise. And you at the heart of it.

RAINEY smiles.

RAINEY: That's lovely. That's a lovely thought.

She drinks.

RAINEY: I remember Dad planting that orchard. And I think – but perhaps I'm pretending to myself – I think I can remember the view down to the sea. You know what was there before the orchard?

VALERIE shakes her head.

RAINEY: Nothing much. Decent pasture, but – a couple of old shepherd's shacks. And Lewis's grandfather lived in one of them. And Dad tried to pay him off but – he wouldn't, you know. So Dad threw him out. Had the place torn down. You can still find the stones, you prod round in the hedges.

VALERIE: So what, according to Rainey Lewis / is doing this –

RAINEY: Your grandfather turfed his grandfather out to plant that orchard. And now he has come to save us. And the only way he can save us, is by tearing the orchard down. That's not what I think. That is – those are facts.

VALERIE: Who would hold a grudge like that, for fifty years?

RAINEY: Any Welshman at all.

And VALERIE stares at her: gives up.

Turns away.

RAINEY: Val?

VALERIE waves her away.

ANYA enters, CERI following her. Wrapped up in each other.

CERI: – honestly, that's all I meant.

ANYA: Honestly, don't flatter yourself.

CERI: Don't often find I need to.

VALERIE finds something to busy herself with.

ANYA: You're so…

CERI: Charming? Irresistible? Enigmatic?

ANYA: Transparent.

CERI, mock-shock places his hand on his heart.

CERI: Ouch!

ANYA: Let me guess, if you had feelings, they'd be hurt.

VALERIE: Oh just shag him, will you.

ANYA: Keep your bony nose out, won't you?

VALERIE: The way you're parading it...

ANYA: It is none of your business whether I'm going to shag him or not.

CERI: Would you mind maybe –

ANYA gets up.

CERI: – telling me?

ANYA heads off.

Pauses. Turns.

ANYA: Come on boy.

And she slaps the front of her thighs – some gesture one would make to summon a dog.

ANYA: Come on, come on boy.

CERI: That's incredibly demeaning.

ANYA: Then sir, I bid you good day.

ANYA turns and goes.

CERI sits there a second. Then –

CERI: Oh balls to it.

And he skedaddles after her.

VALERIE: Bloody look at her.

RAINEY: What if she does screw him?

VALERIE: She only just scraped her end of year exams, I don't want a layabout like him persuading her to drop / out –

RAINEY: She's not going to drop out!

VALERIE: You know what she's like.

RAINEY's not buying it.

VALERIE: Or rather: you don't.

RAINEY: Oh go to hell.

VALERIE stares at her; looks away.

RAINEY relents a bit.

RAINEY: Val.

VALERIE ignores her.

RAINEY: Val don't be boring.

Still no response.

RAINEY: So what will you do when this place is gone? Move in with Lewis?

VALERIE: – so we haven't really thought about it.

RAINEY: But I bet he's thought about it. Where does he live, his dad's cottage?

VALERIE: Rents that out. He's got a new build, just outside Slebech. Ranch style bungalow, views of the estuary.

RAINEY: God how vulgar. Let me guess, swimming pool and double glazing?

VALERIE: Triple, actually.

RAINEY: You're making that up. Imagine this place with double glazing. It'd be almost survivable.

She takes a drink.

RAINEY: Well. I hope you'll be very happy there.

VALERIE: I won't be going there.

RAINEY: No? Good. Do you good to just, live on your own for a bit.

VALERIE: I'll be coming with you.

RAINEY laughs.

RAINEY: I wouldn't have thought / that would be –

VALERIE: What's your plan, Mum? You've sold the flat, living in a hotel – and when the money runs out?

RAINEY: I plan to enjoy myself immensely.

VALERIE: Then I'd better be there, for that.

RAINEY: I don't want you there.

VALERIE: Can't stop me.

RAINEY considers.

Turns, shouts to off.

RAINEY: DOTTIE! *(To VALERIE.)* No, but I can get a head start.

DOTTIE appears. Yellow gloves on up to her arms. Massive spanner in one of her hands.

DOTTIE: And?

RAINEY: Can you get me a taxi darling?

DOTTIE: On a Sunday? Wouldn't have thought so.

DOTTIE trudges off. Stops.

DOTTIE: By the way Val – it's leaking again back bathroom.

VALERIE: Okay, put some / towels [down to soak]

DOTTIE: Yeah I done that. We getting it fixed then?

LEWIS wanders on.

VALERIE: Soon as I can.

RAINEY: Sorry – my taxi?

DOTTIE: *(To RAINEY.)* I'll get it now.

RAINEY: {You're bloody not getting it now…}

DOTTIE: It's gonna ruin that floor.

VALERIE: I said, as soon as I can.

DOTTIE: *(As if VAL has said 'As soon as I can be bothered.')* Okay, it's up to you.

LEWIS: Hey you know there's water coming down the back kitchen wall?

VALERIE: Yes, I'd heard reports.

RAINEY is watching them.

LEWIS: From the back bathroom probably. Get one of the boys out shall I?

VALERIE: Please, could you?

LEWIS looks – from VAL to RAINEY, back.

LEWIS: What's up?

She looks at him: what d'you think?

VALERIE: Nothing.

LEWIS goes to a jug of orange juice. Pours a glass.

LEWIS: Look tired love.

VALERIE: Thanks.

He gives her the juice.

VALERIE: But this'll perk me up!

LEWIS doesn't rise to it: watches her. Then –

LEWIS: Rainey, you was wanting a taxi take you to the station?

RAINEY: If such a wonder might be obtained.

LEWIS: It might, but no point. No trains on a Sunday.

RAINEY: Oh good grief…

LEWIS: 'Salways been like that. Swansea's first place you can get a train on a Sunday.

RAINEY: Force majeure forces my hand.

LEWIS: Sorry what?

RAINEY: I'll stay one more night. Get the train back home tomorrow.

LEWIS: I could run you to Swansea now. Hour there hour back nice little spin.

RAINEY: Well… alright, thank you.

LEWIS: Right. Just change my boots, these are buggers to drive in. You seen my daps Val?

VALERIE: Yes: I tried to burn them. They wouldn't.

VAL goes off to get LEWIS's daps.

LEWIS: You gonna say bye to the place then?

She stares back at him.

RAINEY: Bye, place.

Then –

RAINEY: What?

VALERIE returns, daps in hand.

LEWIS: Cheers love.

VALERIE: Will you ring us when you get back?

RAINEY: I'll mean to.

LEWIS struggles to prise one work boot off his feet with the toe of another.

Gives up, bends to pull the boot off. Recoils.

VALERIE: What?

LEWIS: My damn back...

VALERIE: Just, sit will you.

LEWIS sits down.

VALERIE kneels at his feet.

With some struggle, pulls the boots off his feet.

Puts the daps on.

Ties them up.

VALERIE: Yes.

LEWIS: Yes what?

VALERIE: Yes they bloody honk.

LEWIS: Working man love. Get used to it.

She starts to stand – he offers her his hand. Holds his hand steady, so she can pull herself to her feet. And then stands himself. They end up standing very close, holding hands.

LEWIS: {You alright?}

VALERIE nods.

They look at each other a moment.

And RAINEY is watching all this.

VALERIE and LEWIS break.

LEWIS comes over to RAINEY.

LEWIS: That's us then.

And RAINEY... doesn't know what to do.

RAINEY: Is it?

VALERIE: Mum?

RAINEY: I don't know...

The other two looking at her.

RAINEY: I don't know!

VALERIE: Well if you don't know, then –

LEWIS: So we getting in the car?

RAINEY: Could we? Oh God...

VALERIE: – don't do this, please, it's been too much –

LEWIS: This is us now, come on.

RAINEY: Because I can just remember it, I think. The view down the field. The view down to the sea. I can just remember it, from when I was a little girl. From before the orchard grew. And I never thought I'd see that view again. But let's see it. Let's see how it looks –

VALERIE: Oh Mum...

VALERIE goes to her; stops, very near to her.

LEWIS: I wanna contract signed. Not having you messing me around like you messed Val around.

RAINEY: Of course!

LEWIS: Place is gonna be noisy as hell mind.

RAINEY: I know.

VALERIE: Noisy, and busy, and full.

RAINEY: Yes, yes, yes. To all of it.

And – at first with some awkwardness, but then properly – they hug.

THREE

Days later.

ANYA sits. Hugging her knees to her chest.

CERI's sketching her.

ANYA: I thought all art was bollocks.

CERI: This isn't art, it's drawing.

Little pause.

ANYA: Am I sitting like this much longer?

CERI: Thing with drawing is, unlike "art" you can actually tell if it's good or not, because – does it look like the thing it's supposed to be or not? So you have to put a bit of effort / in –

ANYA: Just I'm starting to cramp.

CERI: I did say sit so's it felt natural.

ANYA: It felt natural at first and / now I'm starting –

CERI: Yeah do what you like. I've got you.

He works, speaks without looking at her.

CERI: And I never said all art was bollocks. Drawing is fine. Pop music is a three minute burst of joyous release from the daily grind. What I said was, any art that has to be explained to you before you get it, is bollocks. It's for rich people to fritter their money on and demonstrate their superiority over the common man.

ANYA: And woman.

CERI: In standard usage man as a general noun is taken to include / woman –

ANYA: They do say lefties are the most chauvinist of all.

CERI: Who says that?

ANYA: Every single Tory boy at uni who tries to get off with me.

CERI: And what d'you tell them?

ANYA: I say, *(Breathlessly.)* yes I'm sure you're right darling...
You finished?

CERI: It's never finished. You just stop.

ANYA: Jesus, can I see it?

He stops.

CERI: I'm shy now.

ANYA: Half an hour ago in my room you were the least shy
I've seen anyone be, ever.

CERI: But drawing you... I'm showing you how I see you.
Letting you in my head.

ANYA: Christ I'm not sure I'm ready for that.

She holds out her hand for the pad. CERI hands it over.

ANYA studies his work.

Looks at him, taking issue.

CERI: What?

ANYA: My boobs are nowhere near that big.

CERI takes the pad. Peers at it. Peers at it again.

CERI: ...those are your knees? Cos you're like – sat with

*He mimes, putting his arms around imaginary knees, hugged into
his chest.*

ANYA: Oh okay right.

She looks again.

ANYA: Oh right so –

She peers sideways at the pad.

ANYA: Well come on they're bigger than *that.*

CERI takes the pad – rips out the page. Rips it up.

ANYA: Don't!

CERI: It wasn't any good.

ANYA: Dramatic little thing, aren't you...

They look at each other.

CERI: 'S a band on at the Queen's Hall? The Revolvers. New wavey with a bit of – you know.

ANYA: I don't know.

CERI: You do. A bit of –

He shakes his fist, bares his teeth.

CERI: Bit of –

He does a little pelvic thrust.

ANYA: Oh gosh.

CERI: Bit of –

He screams, possibly yodels.

CERI: But they're getting signed soon apparently, so I'd quite like to see them before the music industry ruins them.

ANYA: So I'd be driving?

CERI: Nah we could walk it easy. If we'd started… three hours ago.

ANYA: Just I'd quite like a drink.

CERI: Drive home pissed, you must know the way with your eyes closed.

Tiny hesitation before she answers.

ANYA: What about we wander down the orchard? Bring a few bottles?

He wants to go to the gig; but sees the possibilities.

CERI: Yeah okay.

ANYA: Few blankets.

CERI: Cosy.

ANYA: Something to eat.

CERI: I could eat you alive, I reckon.

ANYA: I might let you.

CERI's smiling – the smile vanishes. Something hits him. He tries to bury it.

CERI: Yeah, that'd great, let's head down the [orchard]

He stops.

CERI: I'm really sorry.

ANYA doesn't answer.

CERI: That is so – oh God…

ANYA: 'S okay.

CERI: But – "yeah, just drive home half pissed"?

ANYA: People do.

CERI: Yeah. Yeah well you would know. And I'm thinking about it whenever I'm talking to you, don't mention – don't talk about –

ANYA: Ceri.

CERI: Yes.

She doesn't say anything.

Nor does he for a bit. Then –

CERI: You just wanted me to stop talking.

ANYA: And it worked for a bit.

ANYA gets up. Picks up the torn quarters of the sketch.

ANYA: Can I keep these?

CERI: … [if] you want.

ANYA: I mean you're right it's not an amazing drawing, but stuck back together with sellotape it'll have a pleasing melancholy. I'll put it on my wall back at uni and handsome girls and pretty boys will say – hey. What's the story with *that?*

CERI: I'm really sorry.

ANYA: People say worse.

She looks at him.

ANYA: Go on then. You want to ask about it. Or say things about it. Go on.

CERI: Just – losing your dad that way. And so soon after losing / your [brother]

ANYA: Yes. Wasn't it terribly bad luck.

He smiles at her.

ANYA: It wasn't luck though. You know that don't you?

CERI: You lose your kid. You're gonna – course you're gonna hit the bottle.

ANYA: No.

He looks at her.

ANYA: It wasn't – he didn't drink cos he was… sad and then –

She trails off. Starts again.

ANYA: D'you know where he came off the road?

CERI shakes his head.

ANYA: He was in Narberth. The Eagle, the Angel, stopped for a couple more at the Bush in Canaston Bridge. Said his goodbyes; headed for home. And that stretch in Cresselly? Stone walls right up against the road both sides?

CERI: By the hunt?

ANYA: Yeah. There. Doing between sixty-five and seventy-five, according to the report.

CERI: I'm so sorry. Christ what is the use of saying that?

ANYA: It helps.

CERI: Does it?

ANYA: Every time.

She's waiting for him to get something. He doesn't.

ANYA: The whole drive home. It's hedges. Fields. A river, but not a very deep one. You could come off the road almost anywhere, and walk away from it. The place he comes off, is the one place you will not walk away. He comes off the one place where you will smash into a six foot thick stone wall and –

CERI: That is just the worst possible [luck] –

Her look stops him.

CERI: Oh God.

ANYA: He left us. When we'd just lost Joseph. He got in his car and he never came back.

CERI: You can't be sure that's / how it –

ANYA: Mum is sure. That's why there's nothing left of him in the house. She keeps her wedding ring, round her neck. Which is sort of –

She stops.

ANYA: It's something [at least] – but it's like he never existed.

ANYA stops as DOTTIE wanders in. Looks for something in a few places – drawers, corners, shelves.

ANYA: You lost something?

She stops searching.

DOTTIE: Looking for Val really. Seen Val?

ANYA: Not since this morning. Anything I can help with?

DOTTIE smiles.

DOTTIE: Doubt it.

DOTTIE goes.

ANYA: Yeah let's go to this gig then. And I'll just not drink.

CERI: Then nor will I.

ANYA: Oh no do. You're nicer when you're giggly.

CERI: I am not a giggly drunk. I am moody, little bit dangerous –

ANYA: You are giggly and breathless, like a girl. Or perhaps that's just around me.

CERI: You're very confident of yourself.

ANYA: Thanks so much.

CERI: Rich girls usually are.

ANYA: Well I'd hate to disappoint.

Little pause.

ANYA: You know what. I do want a drink. So let's forget the gig. Let's go down to the orchard. Bring a few blankets. Have a little fire. Get wasted.

CERI: Be a bit cold, won't it.

ANYA: Usually is in March.

CERI: April today.

ANYA: Is it?

CERI nods.

ANYA leans over, gives him a pinch and a punch.

ANYA: ...and no return to me.

CERI: Still be cold though.

ANYA: Sure it will be, as the evening wears on. What will we do to keep warm?

CERI smiles.

ANYA: I'd just like to be there, a bit. Before it all goes. Say goodbye. You think that's ridiculous.

CERI: No...

She can't decide if it's worth going on with him about this.

ANYA: Thing is I was so young, I don't really remember him. Half the things I think I remember I'm not sure if I'm really remembering Joe or if they're things people have told me. But I remember him in the orchard. We'd just wander about there when we were tiny, cos it was safe, no one else around. There was this time we were –

She pauses.

ANYA: – building a dam over the stream and a squirrel darted past and we put down some jam sandwich and it came out again. And it was browny-red. And everyone got really excited because it was a squirrel and it was red and there weren't any of them left any more. And Dad was saying we'd got it wrong it must have been a grey. And Joseph saying no, no it was definitely red. All these grown-ups telling him he was wrong and he would not – and we came down again the next day with more jam sandwiches – like that was what had brought the red squirrel to us? And we stayed, and stayed, no bloody squirrel. And then it got dark. And we were cold. And suddenly the trees were all scary, and – we huddled together and we knew we should go home but we didn't dare move and then – and then Mum and Dad came. Mum picked me up and Dad grabbed Joseph. And I remember – as they carried us through the trees – catching Joe's eye. And I remember it. The rest of it is just stuff, story I've told a dozen times before like I'm saying the words cos those are the words I always say when I tell this story. But that moment. Him looking at me and me looking at him. Me in Mum's arms, him in Dad's. And the trees around us and the moon and the shadows. All of that is in my head, now. All of that – and they're going to tear that place down, cover it with brick and concrete. And fine. Fine, if that's what it takes.

CERI: Then let's go, let's go and be there –

ANYA: No, it'll be weird now.

CERI: If you say so.

She doesn't relent.

CERI: Maybe it will help if you think, having that beautiful place, having that – cos you said, you and Joseph wandered around there on your own, cos it was safe. Cos no-one else was allowed there.

She's staring at him. Does he dare go on?

He does.

CERI: And I know it's hard to lose it but – was it ever fair, that you had that beautiful place just to yourselves?

ANYA: So what you're saying is… Even when I'm being sad about my dead brother, I'm still a spoiled bitch?

CERI: No. Not at all.

ANYA: Cos it really bloody sounds like you are.

CERI: But –

ANYA: …Jesus Christ.

CERI: What is better. That you and your family have a lovely orchard to wander around. Or that a hundred families have homes.

She can't answer. Finds another attack.

ANYA: How come you're so keen on Lewis's house-building scheme?

CERI: Houses are more important than trees.

ANYA: No I mean how come you, a raving communist –

CERI: Anarcho-socialist really but all labels are fascism.

ANYA: – how come you, are in favour of his money-making capitalist scheme.

He looks around.

CERI: See this old bookcase?

ANYA: That antique family heirloom? Yes…

CERI: So back in –

ANYA: Victorian? I dunno.

CERI: – before capitalism really got going they made stuff like this, and it was great, the bloke making it

ANYA: Or the woman.

CERI: In Victorian times?

ANYA shrugs.

CERI: So he's a master craftsman, he crafts this thing with his hands and, I dunno – a plane? A lathe? Not really the carpenting type but – you know it's all very beautiful and meaningful –

ANYA: And it lasts for a hundred years and we can still use it and treasure it today.

CERI: – but as a manufacturing method it's a dead loss. So inefficient hardly anyone can actually afford one. Just nobs like your… great-great-great-grandnob.

ANYA: You really are winning me over, you know that.

CERI: And then, pow, capitalism, the division of labour, you've got bookcases being made out of chipboard on a production line and every bloke – or girl! – on the line is just – nailing in one nail all day long and it is really efficient, everybody can afford one – but so boring for the poor sods doing it. And competition means the process has to get more and more efficient, until finally they do away with workers altogether, because humans get sick and tired so do you know who ends up making the bookcases?

ANYA: Who?

CERI: Robots. Bloody robots. Yes. The relentless pressure of the market creates the technology to free humans from drudgery. But then no-one's got a job any more. Massive social unrest, a little revolutionary prod from yours truly and – capitalism collapses. Something better takes its place.

ANYA: Or something worse.

CERI: So Lewis builds his houses. And it's crap, that they only go to the people who can pay for them. But after capitalism fails, the houses are still there. And we distribute them according to need, not according to money. So I don't hate capitalism. I mean I do but – it's a stage on the journey. Like if you were gonna clear all the crap out of this place, get it all neat and tidy, there'd be a stage / where –

ANYA: It's not crap, it's lived-in.

CERI: There is crap everywhere you look. Like –

He wanders over to a shelf or dresser.

CERI: What is this?

ANYA: Dunno.

CERI: It's a little – ceramic… I don't know.

ANYA: Walrus.

CERI: Who needs a china walrus?

ANYA: I um – I don't know. You're right. Nobody.

CERI: Should probably throw it away then.

He goes to throw it – ANYA grabs it off him, puts it back down.

ANYA: It's just – it's sad for me, losing a beautiful place. I played in those orchards as a kid. Imagined I'd play in them with my kids. Imagined my kids would play in them with theirs; and would remember playing in them with me.

CERI: And I'm saying: you might feel less sad, if you started to feel uncomfortable about having that beautiful thing, when other people didn't.

ANYA: Now I feel sad; and guilty about feeling sad. Shall we get drunk?

CERI: That's how I get through the [day] – ah.

He stops.

CERI: Actually I'm supposed to go and sign on.

ANYA: You sign on? I thought you taught adult literacy?

CERI: Yeah. They don't pay me for it.

ANYA: I love that. Anarcho-socialist, trots along to sign on…

CERI: The dole is the most socialist part of the state, it's not hypocritical at all. Plus I'm usually late signing on so, I'm still screwing with the system.

Checks his watch. Bit alarmed.

CERI: Couldn't give me a lift could you?

She looks at him. Not impressed.

CERI: Just to the three gates. I'll hitch from there.

ANYA picks up car keys from somewhere. Swings them round her finger.

ANYA: Come on then.

She's heading off. CERI follows.

CERI: *(Leaving.)* If you do wanna take me a bit further than the three gates, that'd be amazing…

RAINEY sticks her head into the room.

Once she's sure they are gone, walks in.

She's trying out being in the space. Tentative, cautious.

Then VALERIE calls –

VALERIE: *(From off.)* Mum?

RAINEY's demeanour shifts instantly.

VALERIE: There you are.

RAINEY: Yes.

VALERIE: Um, Lewis says the contract is all ready.

RAINEY: Good. Then have him bring it round.

VALERIE: You don't want to have someone look at it?

RAINEY: Have you looked at it?

VALERIE: A solicitor of your own. Lewis would prefer you did.

RAINEY: He is a stickler, isn't he.

VALERIE: Apparently if there were any problems, you could say you did't understand / what you were signing –

RAINEY: I don't need a solicitor because I can read a contract myself. Have him bring it here. I'll sign.

VALERIE: Okay.

RAINEY: And we need to talk about bedrooms. I can't stay up in the attic. Bloody pigeons on the roof are driving me round the bend. So – I'll have your room.

VALERIE: My room?

RAINEY: And you move into mine. Makes sense: if you're talking about children and –

VALERIE: Could you not –

RAINEY: – what?

VALERIE: Talk about these things as if they're already happening. Because I haven't actually –

RAINEY: Does he not know? That you have him down to marry you and impregnate you and raise the next generation. Because you should tell him; he's going to need to schedule it around his work commitments.

VALERIE: Of course he knows, he – we just haven't discussed it, as such –

RAINEY: You want to get that down in writing – some sort of contract possibly? Shall I ask him?

VALERIE: Please just –

She gives up that thought.

VALERIE: Are you absolutely sure, you don't want your room?

RAINEY doesn't answer.

VALERIE: Mum.

Still nothing.

VALERIE: *Mum.*

RAINEY: *(Quietly.)* I can't.

VALERIE hesitates. Then –

VALERIE: What about your things? I left the room as it was –

RAINEY: Chuck it all in the bin.

VALERIE: What if together we go through your things –

RAINEY: No.

VALERIE: There'll be some things you want to keep?

RAINEY: No.

VALERIE: Mum.

RAINEY: If you're going to have a family, you'll need space for your things. All the things a baby needs, you have no idea.

VALERIE: Maybe we could use some old things. I was digging around in the attic. There are tea chests up there.

RAINEY: Aren't they locked?

VALERIE: I forced the locks. Darling little clothes. Little cardigan. No labels, so hand-knitted I think. Who knitted them?

RAINEY: My mum.

VALERIE: They're beautiful.

RAINEY: She'd never sleep when it was light. So she was late to bed, early to rise all summer through. And she'd sit there, click-clacking away. Have a new warm cardigan ready for the winter. She was half way through knitting one when –

VALERIE: It was summer. When he went.

RAINEY: 'Went.' Good God.

VALERIE: Sorry.

RAINEY: I hate all that. So sorry to hear of your son's passing.

VALERIE: What would you like us to say?

RAINEY: Say nothing. Shut your bloody mouths.

She stops.

RAINEY: He didn't pass, he got *smashed*, he – I'm not even here. I'm a ghost. I'm not here, I'm there. On that beach. I wake up and I know I shouldn't have been asleep and – he's not there and I panic and – there he is. There he is, waving. And I slump down all relieved and then – I see. Those sideways slabs of rock that push up through the sand, out in the middle of the bay. Bigger than a house but the high tide cuts them off. Low tide the pools are always full of fish and crabs and creatures that get trapped when the sea slips away. And Joseph's waded out there. Poking sticks at soft, squidgey things, chasing crabs under stones. He's not noticed the water coming back in around him. Behind him. Not till the rock pools start to bubble and froth. And by then – the water between him and the beach is already deeper than he likes the look of. So he's climbed up to the highest shelf of rock. And he's waving. Waving cos he's scared. And he's been out there – how long. He's been waving to me – how long? While I was asleep. – I run into the water I shout come on, come on, swim, now. But he's too scared. The waves are too big and he's too scared to dive into them and –

GABRIEL: Glorious news! Gather ye round, gather ye round!

VALERIE: Uncle, do / you mind –

GABRIEL: Gather everyone, glad tidings of great joy!

RAINEY retreats slightly.

DOTTIE enters.

GABRIEL: There you are my girl – shall we have a drink?

DOTTIE: Well I don't get off till six, but if you can wait till then...

GABRIEL: Very good, very good – I meant for the uh...

DOTTIE: I know what you meant.

DOTTIE goes about getting drinks.

GABRIEL: Rainey, come along, stop cowering in the corner –

VALERIE: Uncle.

GABRIEL: – this is for you too!

RAINEY moves towards the group.

DOTTIE: What'll you have, Valerie?

VALERIE: Nothing for me thanks.

GABRIEL: I'll have hers!

RAINEY: I'll have hers.

They speak almost in unison.

GABRIEL: Ah-ha! Make a wish, make a wish!

GABRIEL rushes over to her, makes her link pinky fingers, closes his eyes.

GABRIEL: Can you guess what I wished for?

RAINEY: World peace.

GABRIEL: You know me so well! You?

RAINEY: World war.

DOTTIE: But neither of them will come true, because you told.

GABRIEL: Although perhaps I *didn't* wish for world peace.

RAINEY: I definitely wished for world war. Where's my bloody drink.

DOTTIE: What did you wish for then?

GABRIEL: Maybe something more... succulent.

RAINEY: I might go and rest for a while, if no one minds...

GABRIEL: But my announcement!

RAINEY: Ah yes. Of course.

GABRIEL: Ladies and – well, it's just ladies in fact – I have been offered a job!

RAINEY: How did you come to be looking for a job?

GABRIEL: I wasn't looking. It was offered.

VALERIE: What sort of job would someone offer you?

GABRIEL: Working for a bank.

VALERIE: In what capacity?

GABRIEL: I was anticipating congratulations...

DOTTIE: You gonna be behind the counter when I take my coppers in to the Midland, are you?

GABRIEL: Who knows! No it's more the investment side.

VALERIE: What do you know about investment banking?

GABRIEL: Well I don't really understand it, but apparently I don't need to, because I'm not –

VALERIE: Is this an April Fool's joke?

GABRIEL: Is it April Fool's today?

DOTTIE: No.

GABRIEL: Then why'd she / ask –

DOTTIE: April Fool! It actually is!

GABRIEL: Ah very amusing, very droll!

ANYA walks in, takes in the scene.

ANYA: What's all this?

VALERIE: Uncle's got a job.

She smiles. Stops smiling.

ANYA: What really?

GABRIEL: I could get offended if I'd a mind to...

ANYA: It's just hard to imagine you –

RAINEY: I will go for that nap...

VALERIE: Mum...

ANYA: Leave her be, will you, she's obviously exhausted.

RAINEY heads off.

GABRIEL: But Rainey I haven't had chance to tell you –

RAINEY's gone.

GABRIEL: *(After her.)* Right I'll fill you in later!

ANYA: What sort of job?

GABRIEL: Investment banking.

ANYA: Is this an April Fool?

GABRIEL: I think I do have a mind to get offended!

VALERIE: These people, that say they offered you a job – they didn't ask for money, did they? Some sort of... agency fee?

GABRIEL: D'you think I've been duped in some sort of con? What sort of idiot d'you think I am?

VALERIE: ...how is the orangery at your house coming on?

Initially GABRIEL can't speak.

GABRIEL: That young man said he'd be back to finish the job as soon as the parts come into stock, and I believe him.

DOTTIE: So what is this job then?

GABRIEL: It's – there are different currencies. There are. And the currencies trade against one another at different values. And if you have some money in one kind of currency, for example...

He can't think of an example.

VALERIE: Pounds?

GABRIEL: Good, close to home – you can make more pounds by selling your pounds for dollars when the pound is strong; and then selling your dollars for pounds when the pound is weak. You end up with more pounds than you started with, just by throwing your money around.

DOTTIE: See that sounds dodgy to me.

GABRIEL: Gosh no no no no no. No it's all perfectly – that sort of thing is the foundation of the modern financial system apparently. So it's all fine.

VALERIE: But you could lose money? If you got it wrong.

GABRIEL: Well yes except – these clever young men, they've found a way to automate the whole process, so that when the currencies shift in London, their office knows about it in New York, before the actual currency exchanges do. And they only know a couple of seconds faster – but that's all the time the machines need!

VALERIE: Now it really does sound like fraud.

GABRIEL: It sounds like fraud, but it's actually ingenuity.

ANYA: And you're going to work the machines?

GABRIEL: Goodness me no. The clever young men do that.

DOTTIE: You're going to – make tea for the clever young men?

GABRIEL: I tried making tea once – you can still see the burn in the right light. No I leave that to the experts!

He winks jovially at her.

VALERIE: So what are you doing?

GABRIEL: Oh well the young men just need some money to play with. And I may be able to persuade certain wealthy individuals to invest in the scheme –

DOTTIE: But you can't even explain what it is without making it sound like fraud.

GABRIEL: Apparently these wealthy individuals are less concerned about that than you are, Dottie, so – but anyway it's more that I, as a person of a certain background, a certain... *(He tries again.)* You see these young men – they're all computer scientists –

ANYA: And what actually is a computer scientist, Uncle Gabriel?

GABRIEL: Look the whole point is, if things go well, I may have a little bit to contribute to keeping the old family seat above water.

ANYA: That's really good of you, Uncle.

VALERIE: But we've sorted all that out now.

ANYA: Val...

GABRIEL: Even if it's a few pennies – you take care of the pennies.

DOTTIE: My mum always used to say that.

GABRIEL: Wise woman indeed.

DOTTIE: Course she died penny-less.

GABRIEL: Oh.

DOTTIE: Born penniless too so, no loss really.

VALERIE: It's very kind of you, Uncle, but – we have a plan now. We're going to build houses on the orchard, and that's all we need.

GABRIEL: I suppose what I was saying is – I was saying to young Anya, things always come up. And she – well you worried didn't you. So just – you see? Things did come up. My job. And um, this thing with the orchard – that came up too.

VALERIE: It didn't come up, we thought of it.

ANYA: Lewis did.

GABRIEL: But overall I'm right aren't I?

ANYA: You certainly are.

GABRIEL: And even now you're a little bit laughing at me. And I love to see that. I truly do. But I wish that, just for a moment, you might take your old uncle seriously. Because I told you there was no need to worry. But you did worry, didn't you? And I can't bear to see it.

ANYA: Uncle...

GABRIEL: And there was no need at all. Because just perhaps, old uncle Gabe knows a thing or two.

ANYA: Of course you do.

GABRIEL: Now I think I might allow myself a little indulgence as reward…

He gets out a cigar, pats himself down.

GABRIEL: Could you possibly find me some matches, Dottie?

VALERIE: Not in here, please.

GABRIEL: Not what?

VALERIE: The cigar.

GABRIEL: What about it?

VALERIE: I don't want you smoking it in here.

GABRIEL stares at the cigar, as if there's something he's not understood.

GABRIEL: It's a perfectly / normal –

VALERIE: I don't allow smoking in the house.

GABRIEL: Really? Whyever not?

VALERIE: Makes the place smell.

GABRIEL: No it doesn't! Not my place anyway.

DOTTIE: I think it's the fabrics here. Cos they're quite old? In the curtains?

GABRIEL: Oh I see…

He doesn't see, but he'll take the offered escape.

DOTTIE: Why don't I bring you an ashtray. And your drink. Out on to the verandah.

GABRIEL: That's very kind of you.

DOTTIE leads him out.

GABRIEL: *(Just to DOTTIE.)* My house doesn't smell of cigarette smoke does it?

DOTTIE: Why no mun…

She fetches an ashtray – she's following GABRIEL off-stage, him now gone.

DOTTIE: …just farts and cat piss.

ANYA and VALERIE alone.

ANYA: Today then.

VALERIE: Yes. Should be today. Apparently half the battle is getting the contracts typed up without any mistakes. Comma in the wrong place and the whole thing – can you believe that?

ANYA: I suppose contracts have to be absolutely [right] – or you may as well do everything on a handshake.

VALERIE: You can go back on a handshake.

ANYA: Well, I know, I was – very well done, by the way.

VALERIE looks at her –

VALERIE: I'm not trying to take anything off anybody.

ANYA: What I said was, well done.

VALERIE: Well done for what though?

ANYA: Saving this place.

VALERIE: Right. Not taking it over?

ANYA: You're one step away from telling me I can come back whenever I like. And then we do have a problem.

VALERIE: Why would I say that? When it goes without saying?

ANYA: Yes, once you've moved Lewis in and the place is full of your kids and everything's part of all your plans –

They look at each other.

VALERIE: Say the word and I'll go.

ANYA: No. I always wanted to go, you always wanted to / stay –

From off –

LEWIS: Anyone about?

VALERIE: Here.

LEWIS enters, a big thick brown envelope.

LEWIS: Got everything, at last. Where's your mum?

ANYA: Having a nap.

LEWIS: Is that quick twenty winks nap or half a bottle of vodka nap?

ANYA: She'll be up in a bit.

ANYA leaves.

LEWIS: You alright?

VALERIE: Yes thank you.

LEWIS goes over, kisses her on the top of the head.

LEWIS: Exciting day.

VALERIE: Yeah.

LEWIS gets out a packet of fags.

VALERIE: I had an idea, one thing we might think about.

LEWIS: What's that?

He's getting out a cigarette, patting down for a lighter.

VALERIE: You know what people are eating a lot of now? Yoghurt.

LEWIS: Yoghurt? Are they?

VALERIE: Loads. Wherever someone's selling milk, they're selling yoghurt. This Ski stuff.

LEWIS: Alright.

VALERIE: Strawberry, rhubarb –

LEWIS: Strawberry yoghurt?

VALERIE: Lots of different flavours.

LEWIS: So it doesn't just taste of yoghurt?

VALERIE: It tastes of strawberry, or / whatever –

LEWIS: No I can see you'd need that cos yoghurt tastes of bugger all really.

VALERIE: Well, people are buying it, and it all comes from Germany, Switzerland, places like that.

LEWIS: They eat all sorts of weird crap over there.

VALERIE: But all you really need, to make yoghurt, is milk.

LEWIS: Ham for breakfast. Who'd have ham for breakfast?

VALERIE: Pig meat for breakfast, imagine.

LEWIS: No I take your point. So you're saying, if people are eating yoghurt, let's make yoghurt. We got the milk – we can get strawberries –

Tries to light the cigarette, lighter won't spark.

VALERIE: So it might be worth thinking about?

He stops – becomes aware of his cigarette.

LEWIS: Oh balls you hate this don't you? I'll nip outside.

LEWIS is heading off.

VALERIE: But what d'you reckon?

LEWIS: No I get it, it's a gap isn't it but food production, I don't know the basics, you know, I'd be best off sticking with construction.

VALERIE: I meant it'd be something for me to do.

He looks at her.

LEWIS: Oh. Alright.

He's moving off again.

LEWIS: Be two secs.

VALERIE: I don't mind the cigarette.

LEWIS: Ah you do though. You say you don't now but time will pass and then –

LEWIS changes his mind, puts away the cigarette. Comes back to her.

LEWIS: You could do it.

VALERIE: D'you think so? I've never run a business or worked anywhere –

LEWIS: You run this place. It's the same really – money in, money out.

VALERIE: I suppose.

LEWIS: Look at me. My family are ditch-diggers and road-layers. Didn't stop me. I just had a go. Now I build things. Maggie Thatcher's dad's a grocer. Didn't stop her.

VALERIE: Maybe it should've done.

LEWIS: Can tell your sister's home. *(Beat.)* I'm not gonna say to you, you can do anything you want. None of us can. But I think we can all do, more than we think we can. So do I think you could make some bloody yoghurt? Yes I do!

He puts the cigarette back in the his fag packet for later.

LEWIS: One thing though. Starting a business – it takes you over. There's so much to do – things you could never have thought of, up they come and they've gotta be done and they've gotta be done now.

VALERIE: That's half the fun of it.

LEWIS: Well it is now you say. You know you've earned your pint at the end of the day when the end of the day is three in the morning. But it doesn't leave you with much for anything else.

VALERIE: Anything like what?

LEWIS: Anything else you might want to do. Anything else that might take you over.

VALERIE: No, I know.

LEWIS: *(Not immediately.)* You think you do.

They smile at each other.

LEWIS: You ever cut down a tree?

VALERIE: Never.

LEWIS: Let's go and cut one down. In the orchard. They're coming down anyway.

VALERIE: What for?

LEWIS: Because.

VALERIE: That's not an answer.

LEWIS: Because... a tree's bigger than you. This huge thing. Stands up to wind, stands up to storms. Probably live longer than you will. But you go at it, with your axe. You keeping chopping away. And you can bring this whole huge thing down.

VALERIE: Let's just let the men do it.

LEWIS: We'll pick a tree, the two of us. Bring it down together. And we can get it chopped up. Let it season a bit. Get it sawn and planed into planks. And then give it to my brother. He can make some thing for us.

VALERIE: What sort of thing?

LEWIS: Whatever we want. Table, stool. Cot.

She looks at him.

He looks back.

LEWIS: So long's applewood's good for furniture he might say it's / not –

VALERIE: Okay then.

LEWIS: Yeah?

VALERIE: Yeah, let's go.

VALERIE grabs her coat. They leave.

The weather shifts. Trees outside sway in a squall of wind. The house rattles and creaks.

ANYA comes on.

The wind dies.

Sits in a chair, almost experimentally.

Looking at the place like it's new to her.

Then –

– an air raid siren wails.

Birds call in alarm and warning, take to the wing, fly, still calling to one another.

RAINEY appears.

ANYA: *(Voice slightly raised.)* It's alright, it's just a test.

RAINEY: Well I rather / presumed –

ANYA: They've been doing it the last year, once a week. It's the air base at Brawdy.

RAINEY: That's a way for the sound to carry.

ANYA: I think that's – I think it's supposed to carry.

The siren deepens, slows, falls silent.

ANYA: Course you think it's a test... but you never know. I mean you *do* know, cos if it was for real it'd've been the papers, tensions rising between the White House and the Kremlin that sort of thing – but every time I hear it, I think – what if it wasn't a test? What if the missiles are in the air? These might be our last seconds, just we don't know it. This might be my last breath. Or this. Or this –

RAINEY: Anya –

ANYA: I think if it was real, we'd be radioactive ash by now. We're safe.

RAINEY: No we're not.

ANYA looks at her.

RAINEY: Every second is like that. Every breath.

ANYA doesn't want to hear what RAINEY is telling her.

ANYA: As it happens there was I thing I had to [tell you] – ah yes Lew brought the contract.

RAINEY: Good of him.

ANYA: I think it needs to be done today.

RAINEY: Then let's do it.

ANYA's taking papers out of the envelope.

ANYA: Not a short document then.

RAINEY comes and sits near her. ANYA finds a pen.

RAINEY: Where do I sign?

ANYA scans the document.

ANYA: Here. And here. And – right it says you need to a sign in the presence of a witness.

RAINEY: I've got you, haven't I.

ANYA: Yeah.

RAINEY picks up the pen; peers at the document.

Is about to sign.

ANYA: I'm just wondering... is it alright for me to be a witness? Because I'm family?

RAINEY: Does it matter?

ANYA: I'm saying I think it might. You know what Lewis is like. Bit of a stickler.

RAINEY: So your suggestion is...

ANYA: Perhaps we should wait / until –

RAINEY: You said it needed doing today...

ANYA: It does, or they'll auction the place this afternoon, but done right in half an hour will be fine. And done wrong now, will not.

RAINEY: *(Calm.)* What a tone to use with your mother.

ANYA: I've been using this tone with you for years. You've not been in a state to notice.

RAINEY turns away from her.

RAINEY: I'm exhausted.

ANYA: I thought you just had a nap.

RAINEY: Just lay there.

ANYA: Let me get you a blanket.

She goes to a blanket box. There's crap all over it. Tries to open the box a crack, pull the blanket out.

RAINEY: That won't work / you know –

The crap on top of the blanket box tips on floor.

RAINEY: There we are.

ANYA brings the blanket to RAINEY, tucks her in.

Goes back to the blanket box.

Picks up the crap.

Doesn't know what to do with it and now has her hands too full to clear space.

RAINEY watches her.

ANYA pushes the blanket box open with her foot.

Drops all the crap into the box.

Shuts the box.

ANYA: Nothing seems so bad with clear surfaces.

RAINEY laughs.

ANYA: It's nice to see you laugh nicely. Not sneering at someone.

RAINEY: I actually was laughing at you.

ANYA: Yes but not in an awful way, so…

They sit.

ANYA: Do you need anything?

RAINEY looks at her. Laughs again.

ANYA: Okay, that is getting tiresome…

ANYA moves away. Fiddles with bits and bobs on a dresser or chest of drawers.

ANYA: You know what I think will be lovely about having you back.

RAINEY looks at her.

ANYA: Not lovely then. But good. Good in the way exercise is good, or muesli is good –

RAINEY: Oh, good in the way that all sane people hate.

ANYA: Yes, that exactly.

ANYA hesitates.

ANYA: I think, that you being back here –

RAINEY knows instantly the territory ANYA's heading into.

ANYA: There's still more of him. We lost him but – there
are bits you don't know about and the more we're here
together the more will come back to me. Like this –

She picks up the ceramic walrus CERI picked out.

RAINEY: What on earth is it?

ANYA: It's… a ceramic walrus.

RAINEY: Oh wonderful. What a treasure.

ANYA: Do you know where it came from? Do you know why
it's here?

RAINEY looks at her.

ANYA: Mum.

RAINEY: He got it for me.

ANYA: Yes. Do you know where?

RAINEY: How would I / know that –

ANYA: It was Manor House. We went on a school trip. I
remember because it was the first school trip I ever went
on, and I remember you telling Joe he had to look after
me and be a big brother to me. Little git barely spoke
to me the whole day. I remember having a Mini Milk
and dropping it on the floor and picking it up and it
was covered in gravel and I cried. And Joe saw, kept on
playing with his friends. And I remember the end of the
day we could go to the shop to spend our spending money.
Or there was this little pond, with boats, with these remote
control boats you put your fifty pee in and you could drive
them round the pond for a minute. And they were the best
thing. Everyone put every fifty pee they had into these
boats. But not Joe. He really wanted to, but he didn't. He
went to the shop. To get something for you. But he had
no idea what. And he had his pound. And I remember
him finding things that were a pound. This little walrus
and – something else I don't remember. And he picked
up this little walrus, looked at it, put it down, picked up
the other thing. And was there for – picking up this walrus
and putting it down. Trying to decide what would be the

best thing for you. Trying to decide what would make you happy. And not having a clue. This crappy little thing –

She puts the walrus down in front of RAINEY.

ANYA: Did you know that? Did you know any of that?

RAINEY doesn't answer.

ANYA: Mum.

RAINEY: No.

ANYA: Well there you are.

From off – an axe, striking a tree.

ANYA: What the hell is that?

And again. And again.

ANYA: I'll go and see.

She flees.

RAINEY sits.

The room tone grows.

From the side of stage, a little wooden toy truck trundles on.

The axe still falling.

RAINEY gets up.

Approaches the truck as it were an animal that might bite her, or might run off.

Picks it up.

Stands with it, not knowing what to do.

And then puts it down on the floor.

Rolls it back to where it came from.

The axe stops.

Almost instantly ANYA appears.

ANYA: Right, that was –

Something about RAINEY makes her stop.

ANYA: You alright?

RAINEY gestures to a bottle of wine.

RAINEY: Could you pour me a glass love?

ANYA walks over.

Picks up the bottle.

ANYA: It's empty.

RAINEY: You sure.

ANYA: Absolutely.

ANYA puts the bottle behind her back.

RAINEY stares at her.

RAINEY: Plenty more in the kitchen.

ANYA: Mum –

RAINEY strides off.

VALERIE enters.

VALERIE: Where is she?

ANYA looks at her, doesn't answer.

VALERIE: You said Mum was up, where is she? An?

ANYA puts down the bottle.

ANYA: She's gone.

INTERVAL.

FOUR

RAINEY stands alone. Wine glass in hand.

She's building up to something.

RAINEY: DOTTIE!

From off –

DOTTIE: COMING!

RAINEY: You said you were getting me a drink and I haven't –

RAINEY notes the full glass in her hand. Downs it.

RAINEY: – got a drink so what the hell's going on.

DOTTIE arrives with bottle and glass.

DOTTIE: I'm sure I *did* get you a drink you know…

RAINEY: Then where is it?

RAINEY puts the empty glass behind her back.

DOTTIE moves to a table where she can put down the bottle and glass.

As DOTTIE's back is turned, RAINEY stuffs the glass under the cushion of the nearest chair to DOTTIE.

DOTTIE pours a glass. Turns to hand it to RAINEY.

RAINEY: Finally.

DOTTIE holds back from handing over the glass.

DOTTIE: Why don't you sit down to enjoy it?

RAINEY: Might thanks.

RAINEY moves towards a different seat.

DOTTIE: That's the nicest chair.

RAINEY: Is it.

DOTTIE: Go on. Sit in the nicest chair with this lovely glass of wine. Spoil yourself.

RAINEY: I can't.

DOTTIE: Why?

RAINEY: Smells of sick.

DOTTIE loses patience, fetches glass out from under cushion.

DOTTIE: You're a bloody disgrace.

RAINEY: Ooh thanks, I will put my feet up as it happens.

RAINEY plops herself down.

DOTTIE: Have you signed that contract?

RAINEY: Got hours yet.

DOTTIE: You've got *an* hour. Then the auction.

DOTTIE heads off.

RAINEY: Leave the bottle!

DOTTIE: Miss Valerie told me not to leave a bottle with you.

RAINEY: I love it when you get all below stairs...

DOTTIE keeps heading off.

RAINEY: And you're actually going to do what she said?

DOTTIE: Looks like it.

RAINEY: You're sacked. Get out now.

DOTTIE: Top up before I put it back in the pantry?

RAINEY: Oh thanks ever so.

DOTTIE strides off.

RAINEY: Bless you darling.

GABRIEL enters.

GABRIEL: Wonderful, you've surfaced.

RAINEY shrinks in her chair.

RAINEY: Dive dive dive!

GABRIEL: *(To off.)* She's in here!

RAINEY: No she's not!

GABRIEL: I thought I might I tell you about my new job!

RAINEY: Goodness me why.

GABRIEL: It's quite big news, for me, / branching out into –

RAINEY: Before you really dig in could you just get me a little drink darling?

GABRIEL: By all means, what will you [have]

He peers at her: sees her drink.

GABRIEL: You've already got one, you old lush…

She takes a sip.

RAINEY: No I haven't.

GABRIEL: I can see it in your [hand] –

RAINEY: See what? Have you got your glasses on?

GABRIEL brings his hand right to his face and feels around where his glasses might be.

GABRIEL: Actually no.

RAINEY: Then there's the problem. And I haven't got a drink, that's the other / problem –

GABRIEL: Yes, alright…

GABRIEL heads off.

RAINEY takes a congratulatory swig, pleased with herself.

From off –

VALERIE: Mum?

RAINEY: Oh God…

She finishes the glass, in a couple of swift swigs.

VALERIE: There you are.

LEWIS arrives. He has the contract.

VALERIE: Now please pay attention.

RAINEY: Why does she talk to me like I'm a four year old?

LEWIS: If I answer that, you and me are gonna fall out.

RAINEY: *(Mock Welsh accent, deep voice.)* Wossat ew say there Lewis?

He gets the contract out.

LEWIS: Come on then.

RAINEY takes the pen.

Takes the top off.

Inspects the document.

Relishes the moment.

RAINEY: There is just one *teensy-weensy* sticking point, as I see things.

VALERIE: Oh, Mum...

LEWIS: This is not the time to try driving a hard bargain.

RAINEY lets him finish.

RAINEY: I have been asking for hours it seems, for a drink. And nobody has got me one. I'm not signing, till there's a drink in my hand.

GABRIEL walks on with a drink.

GABRIEL: There you go.

He puts the drink in her hand.

RAINEY: Thanks darling – take my empty for me?

She's offering him her empty glass – GABRIEL looks at it, a bit confused – then abandons his confusion.

GABRIEL: But of course.

VALERIE: So?

RAINEY: Mmm?

VALERIE: So now you've got your drink.

RAINEY: Ah yes. Do you know – I think now I'd like a smoke.

VAL and LEWIS talk over one another.

VALERIE: You / can have a fag, once you've signed.

LEWIS: No smoking in here, Val doesn't like it.

RAINEY: Sorry what?

LEWIS: You can have a fag, after you've signed – but outside.

RAINEY: Or –

She gets to her feet.

RAINEY: – possibly, I could wander outside and have a fag now?

She moves, experimentally, off.

RAINEY: Yes look. It seems that's entirely possible!

RAINEY goes.

LEWIS: She's not gonna sign.

VALERIE: She will…

LEWIS: She's been dicking us around this whole time. I'm gonna look a bloody idiot – d'you know how much solicitors charged me for this?

VALERIE: You have mentioned, once or twice…

GABRIEL: Of course she's going to sign. She's just… enjoying her moment.

VALERIE: You're sure?

DOTTIE enters. Waits with no good grace while GABRIEL talks.

GABRIEL: Absolutely certain. No doubt at all, she'll do the right thing, if I know my sister – and, word to the wise, I do. *(Little pause.)* Of course I've barely seen her for donkey's years and people do change *(Off their looks.)* I'm joking, I'm joking with you, goodness me you touchy lot…

He turns to DOTTIE.

GABRIEL: Sorry Dottie did you want something?

DOTTIE: No no you just carry on.

GABRIEL: Well I'd finished.

DOTTIE: Am I getting supper for the lot of you or what?

VALERIE: Yes, please.

DOTTIE: So what then?

VALERIE: Hard to think of something everyone'll eat.

DOTTIE: Yeah I know. Shall I just wander into town, have a see what I can / find?

LEWIS: Pantry bare, is it?

DOTTIE: No.

LEWIS: What you buying more for then?

DOTTIE: *(To VAL.)* I'll head off, is it?

LEWIS: Why don't you, go to the pantry, have a good look, and then see what you can make with what you've already got.

DOTTIE: Who d'you think you are?

VALERIE: Actually Dottie, that might not be / such a bad [idea]

DOTTIE: Oh no, okay, that's fine. I'll just... use my imagination, shall I?

This is a threat.

VALERIE: Okay yeah.

DOTTIE: Alright then.

DOTTIE sweeps off.

LEWIS: Why on earth d'you put up with her?

VALERIE: Put up with her how?

LEWIS: She talks to you like you're shit on her shoe.

GABRIEL: That's just her unique charm.

LEWIS: She goes off, I've seen in Jack Williams, she buys what she likes on your money and I bet half of it goes home with her.

VALERIE: She's been with us since she was a girl.

LEWIS: Yeah, she's had a good old run.

GABRIEL: When you're a little more used to having people as part of your household, who are also to put it bluntly paid to be there –

LEWIS: If one of my men even looked at me the way she looks at you, he'd be out on his arse.

GABRIEL: Your men are, with respect, not our Dottie. And their arses are not hers either!

LEWIS: You wanna make this place work, before you go on thinking about yoghurt or whatever Swedish nonsense, you think about controlling costs firsts.

VALERIE: Meaning what exactly?

LEWIS: Meaning, what does she actually do, you couldn't
do yourself? Specially if your mum's moving back. What
d'you need a housekeeper for?

GABRIEL: Yes, now – things are never quite quite as / simple
as that –

LEWIS: Gabriel.

GABRIEL: What?

LEWIS: Button it will you.

GABRIEL stiffens.

GABRIEL: Well I am terribly sorry, if I've offended.

He stalks off.

LEWIS: Who's being the old woman now?

VALERIE: When things were very difficult, Dottie – there were
weeks when she barely went home.

LEWIS: You pay her overtime for that?

VALERIE: I don't know.

LEWIS: And I suppose it's a bit late now –

VALERIE: She wasn't doing it to get overtime, she was doing it
/ because she –

LEWIS: But if you had paid her overtime, you wouldn't feel
so bad about getting rid of her now, would you? And fair
play you're probably right too. If you've just been paying
her for being a housekeeper when actually she hasn't kept
house – she's kept all of you.

VALERIE takes this in.

VALERIE: I'll just go and see that she's alright.

VAL's moving off.

LEWIS: Course she's alright…

LEWIS left alone.

And once left alone, he stands.

Looks round the place. Considers. Comes to a conclusion.

LEWIS: D'you know, you bloody could.

Near the front of the stage is outside. A patch of garden near the house, or a verandah. ANYA and CERI are lounging in the sun. With them, a record player and a pile of records.

ANYA shows him a record.

CERI: No.

Another.

CERI: No.

A third.

CERI: Gimme that.

ANYA: Why?

CERI: I'm gonna set fire to it.

She puts the record away. Picks up another one. Puts it one.

CERI: What's that?

She shrugs.

The record starts.

It's 'Geno', by Dexy's.

ANYA's looking at him. Well?

CERI: Yeah okay.

ANYA: Okay?

He nods.

They look at each other. ANYA's smiling. CERI's smirking.

CERI: What?

ANYA: You're such an idiot.

Raising his voice over the music –

CERI: Sorry can't hear cause of the –

ANYA gets to her feet.

CERI: Oh okay.

She starts to move.

ANYA: Come on.

CERI: No.

ANYA: You don't dance?

CERI: I'm not dancing.

ANYA: Not even with me?

CERI: Well if I'm not dancing, then I'm not dancing with you or anyone else, am I.

ANYA: So you *can't* dance.

CERI: Didn't say that.

ANYA: You know who doesn't dance? Virgins.

CERI: Oh really.

She nods.

CERI: Do you think I'm twelve? Do you think I'm just gonna leap up to prove myself? Like a twelve year old?

She keeps dancing, looking right at him.

He leaps up to prove himself. She's delighted.

They dance. They don't touch each other. They are giggling at each other a lot, and not afraid to be silly.

They are sexy as hell.

RAINEY wanders up.

RAINEY: Hello, young people.

ANYA spins out of her dance.

ANYA: Hello, old person.

RAINEY: I'd give you a clip round the ear for that, but I'm on the scrounge.

CERI flips the top off a bottle, hands it to her.

RAINEY: Oh cheers. Was actually after a fag, but now you mention it I'm dying for a drink too.

She takes a swig.

RAINEY: Bloody hell – what is this?

CERI: What does it taste like it is?

RAINEY: It tastes like – stuff you put in the car to stop it, you know. In the winter.

CERI: Antifreeze.

RAINEY: Yes.

ANYA: How d'you know what antifreeze tastes like?

ANYA's handing her a packet of cigarettes.

RAINEY: Oh darling: let's not be coy.

RAINEY offers one to CERI.

CERI: No thanks. The only drug that passes my lips is dexedrine.

RAINEY: The pill that saved a nation!

ANYA doesn't get the reference.

CERI: They gave it to pilots in the Battle of Britain, so they could keep on flying.

ANYA: Really?

RAINEY: Your grandfather still had some official RAF issue dexies when I was a little girl. He'd pop one when he had to do a long drive down here from London. He'd pack us into the boot of the car in a bundle of blankets, we'd set off – and then we'd wake. And we'd be here. And he'd still be whistling away…

ANYA: What about booze, you put enough of that away.

CERI: Booze is not a drug. It is a necessity of surviving late capitalism.

RAINEY: Cheers to that.

They clink bottles. Drink. RAINEY takes a long drag of her cigarette.

Stubs it out.

RAINEY: There we are. My last cigarette. Until the next one.

She gets up.

RAINEY: As you were, young people.

She wanders off.

CERI: I'd forgotten how much I like her.

ANYA: Honestly…

ANYA picks another record. Shows it CERI.

CERI: Gimme that, I'm gonna smash it.

She gives it to him.

He breaks it in two.

ANYA: You / arsehole!

CERI: What is really annoying is, they used to be good. I remember them doing sessions on John Peel and they tore holes in the sky and then – get signed, sell out, turn shite.

ANYA: I quite like it.

CERI: Well, I'm sure you're supposed to.

He swigs.

CERI: You know at the dole they're starting these schemes they want you to go on, make it look like you're not on the dole, so they can say unemployment is down.

ANYA: Right…

CERI: And one of the schemes is called… the Enterprise Allowance Scheme. The idea is – you say you're setting up a business. Any business. They pay you, like you were on the dole – but they stop hassling you to get a job. And I said so what – *any* business? And they said yeah. And I said – so what if I said I wanted to start a record label? And they said – great here's the forms.

ANYA: You're starting a record label?

CERI: Like can you imagine if I did? For a laugh? And you wouldn't have to care about selling records so you could just let the bands actually make beautiful music. *(Takes a drink.)* I say beautiful I mean aggressive, disconcerting, revolutionary propaganda in the shape of a three minute pop single / but

ANYA: So why don't you?

CERI: Uh, cos I don't know the first thing / about –

ANYA: So what?

CERI: It would fall apart in six months.

ANYA: So what?

He hasn't got an answer.

ANYA: You said capitalism makes the things we need for a better future and then collapses. So start your record label. Make beautiful music. And let it fall apart.

He hasn't got an answer.

ANYA: Do it. Bloody do it.

CERI: Thing is… you need a thousand quid to put into it to start?

ANYA: You can't get your hands on a thousand quid, from somewhere?

CERI: Amazingly no.

ANYA: Even if you really had to?

CERI: Mork calling rich girl: normal people can't just get their hands on a thousand quid, no.

ANYA flicks through the records. Picks one out. 'Reward' by Teardrop Explodes.

CERI: See these were good, before anyone'd heard of them.

ANYA: Hannah loves this one.

CERI: Who's Hannah?

ANYA looks at him.

CERI: Sorry, should I – who is she?

ANYA: My girlfriend.

CERI: Oh. Yeah. You…

He takes a swig.

CERI: You know if you get to be president of America, you're always president from then on? That's your title. Even when you're not actually the president any more.

ANYA: Okay.

CERI: Is that how it works with being your girlfriend? Once you get the job that's your title from then on. Even after you stop –

ANYA looks at him.

CERI: Not ex-girlfriend?

ANYA: Why would you think she'd be that?

CERI: Because we're –

ANYA: What?

CERI: People mess round at university. Try things out.

ANYA: That's the point of the place. And that's what you assumed I was doing, with her. Messing around. Whereas with you... it's serious.

CERI: So what am I – a summer fling?

ANYA doesn't answer.

CERI: Oh bloody hell. I'm a summer fling!

She smiles.

CERI: I'm ten years older than you!

ANYA: Ten?

CERI: Or so.

ANYA: Oh don't look like that...

CERI: I bloody will look like that.

ANYA: But you know I'm going back to uni. What did you think we would do some sort of long [distance] –

He looks at her.

ANYA: Oh God.

CERI: This is typical, of the monied land-owning classes, treating the proletariat as objects to be / used and thrown –

She laughs at him.

ANYA: Proletariat – look at you!

CERI: Political consciousness does not alienate me from my proletarian roots.

ANYA: You tell them that down the rugby club, do you?

CERI: I fit in very well down the rubgy club, thank you.

ANYA: So – how did you see us working? In the long term?

CERI: We have fun!

ANYA: Yes. That's right. We've had a fun summer fling. But – look at the way you live.

CERI: What about it?

ANYA: I've got things I want to do. Things I want to achieve. You're all over the place.

CERI: How d'you mean?

ANYA: You're on the dole. And you can't get to sign on. You have to hitch.

CERI: Didn't hitch last time.

ANYA: Because I gave you a lift!

CERI: So I didn't hitch.

ANYA: Hannah came up to me in the library one day and just put down, in front of me, two first class air tickets to Stockholm.

CERI: Bit showy.

ANYA: Have you ever travelled first class on a plane?

CERI: I never will, until it's available to every working man. And woman.

ANYA: It is like going to heaven. It is [extraordinary] – and she said, separate rooms when we get there, of course. So I went. And when we got there – four star hotel.

CERI: Oh, you not worth a five?

ANYA: Absolutely beautiful. And we got up to our rooms – except there was only one. Double room. Hannah sat down on this bed and said – if you want to just go home, we can –

CERI: Liar as well as a show-off then.

ANYA: – and I realised, I didn't want to go home. I wanted to stay. So I did. And probably it is just a uni thing. But Ceri. You. Life just batters you about.

CERI: So all your education. All your women's libbing. And all you really want, is a bloke with the cash to sweep you off your feet. Just your bloke might be a girl.

ANYA gives up talking. Finds a record. Puts it on.

It's 'Jealous Guy' by Roxy Music.

CERI: Oh ha bloody ha.

She gets to her feet.

ANYA: *(Cockney geezer accent.)* Come on sweetheart, gimme a dance.

CERI: No.

ANYA: We're here, right now. You can sit, and you can sulk. Or you can hold me. Up to you.

CERI: Don't do slow dancing.

ANYA: You'll be alright. I'll lead.

He gets up. Looks at her.

They fold into one another.

Another part of the stage. A landing.

RAINEY standing, drinking.

She hears someone approach.

Slumps so she's leaning against something or sitting on the floor.

LEWIS arrives.

LEWIS: There you are.

RAINEY: Yes. Wherever I go. There I am.

LEWIS: What's that?

The bottle.

RAINEY: I think it's supposed to be cider. *(Takes a swig.)* I fear for my internal fauna. And my internal organs.

LEWIS: Are you coming to sign.

RAINEY: Yes, alright.

LEWIS: It needs to be done in the next… hour or so.

RAINEY: Next hour and how long, precisely? You know, don't you.

LEWIS: Next hour and twelve minutes. Assuming the auction starts on time.

RAINEY: That gives us plenty of time then. What could go wrong.

LEWIS: Nothing, but still, let's not mess around.

RAINEY: I know what you're doing.

LEWIS: D'you need a hand to get up?

RAINEY: My grandfather threw your grandfather out of his cottage to plant that orchard. So now you're tearing the orchard down.

LEWIS: It's an old country. You dig, you're digging up somebody's bones.

They look at each other.

RAINEY: Tight then. Did I say tight then? Right then. Right then. Let's get this done.

RAINEY hauls herself to her feet – and sort of pushes too hard, staggers. LEWIS has to catch her.

They pull apart.

RAINEY smooths herself down.

RAINEY: Why thank you very much.

She looks at him.

LEWIS: Shall we go then?

RAINEY: You know what I remember? Six months after my husband died. Your dad was doing a job. Anya'd swung on the pantry door, pulled it off its hinges. I got up, middle of the afternoon. Ran a bath. Had a soak. Realised I hadn't brought towels in. So I took the hand towel. Wrapped it round my waist. The corners just met, if I held them in my hand. Walked back to my bedroom and met – you. Here. And we looked at one another. You – a hammer in your hand? And me – just that little towel round my waist. Still wet from the bath. And I stood. And you looked. And you took one step towards me. And I didn't move. And if you'd taken a second step, and a third – I would have let you. My God, I'd have let you. But you ran back down the stairs. A frightened little boy.

She breaks the moment.

RAINEY: Come on then. Let's go and sign on the dotted line!

And she strides off.

LEWIS after her.

In the living room, VALERIE and GABRIEL.

GABRIEL: And in a hundred years – this might be a whole new village.

VALERIE: D'you think?

GABRIEL: It'll be marvellous.

RAINEY enters.

RAINEY: Dottie!

LEWIS follows her.

GABRIEL: You took your time.

LEWIS: Not so you'd notice.

RAINEY: DOTTIE!

GABRIEL: Well, we *did* notice, that's why I'm saying –

DOTTIE enters.

RAINEY: Ah, Dottie darling, could you possibly get me a –

RAINEY's demeanour shifts. She staggers towards a chair.

She grunts – points at a bin.

DOTTIE: You want…

Grunts and points again.

DOTTIE: Oh God!

DOTTIE grabs the bin and shoves it in front of RAINEY's face just in time for her to puke into it.

But RAINEY swallows it back.

RAINEY: I'm fine, I'm fine, I'm fine.

DOTTIE: Swallow it back down?

RAINEY: It's a sin to waste wine. Or antifreeze.

Hands DOTTIE the bin.

RAINEY: Anyway Dottie darling, could you possibly get me a drink? I've a rather unpleasant taste in my mouth, all of a sudden.

She turns to LEWIS.

RAINEY: Yes and where's this contract?

LEWIS finds the place she needs to sign in the contract.

RAINEY: Sorry for keeping you, lovely people. Lewis and I were having a little chat.

LEWIS is approaching her, contract and pen in hand. RAINEY staggers again, and LEWIS has to catch her. She hangs on to him.

RAINEY: Why don't you tell everyone, Lewis, what we were talking about. Why don't you tell Valerie.

He stops.

LEWIS: Alright then.

She smiles at him.

LEWIS: You can't do this.

VALERIE: What's going on?

LEWIS: She's too drunk. She can't sign.

VALERIE: She's got to.

LEWIS: She signs, bank cancels the auction, and a week from now she'll be saying she had no idea what she was signing, cos she was hammered. And she'll get away with it. She'll keep us hanging on, and on. And she is never gonna sell that orchard.

GABRIEL: Then let her sober up – Dottie, black coffee, and plenty of it!

VALERIE: The auction's in an hour.

RAINEY: I'm *fine*.

LEWIS: You are not.

She moves towards him, reaches for the contract. He backs away.

RAINEY: Give it to me.

She advances on him, grabs for it. He gives her a little shove.

VALERIE: Lew!

GABRIEL: Now you steady on, / young man.

RAINEY: I'm going to sign that thing, whether you like it or not –

RAINEY lunges for the contract, gets hold of it.

LEWIS tries to pull it away from her, but she won't let go.

The contract rips.

VALERIE: What are you doing?

GABRIEL: It's all perfectly [fine], we get another copy of the contract –

VALERIE: It took half a day to type that one!

ANYA and CERI arrive, attracted by the commotion.

RAINEY is pouring herself another drink, collected again.

GABRIEL: Then we um we um ummm/mmm –

LEWIS: You know she was never gonna sell that orchard. She was never gonna let rubbish like me live on her doorstep.

VALERIE: She was, till you stopped her! What's going to happen to us?

GABRIEL: Well it um, it looks as if the auction will go ahead.

VALERIE: Yes I [know that] – shut *up*, Uncle Gabe!

She turns on LEWIS.

VALERIE: What have you done?

LEWIS: Me? It was *her*.

He means RAINEY; who is standing, calm and collected, drink in hand.

LEWIS turns to VALERIE.

LEWIS: I'm gonna sort this out.

LEWIS goes.

ANYA: Sorry what's uh, what's going on?

DOTTIE: All that deal to sell the orchard – not happening now.

ANYA: So what's happening to Bloumfield?

GABRIEL: Well the auction's starting in – *(Checks his watch.)* – you never quite know with these things whether they run to time, / people can be very…

ANYA: We're going to lose the whole house? Everything?

It's directed at VALERIE. Everyone looks at her for an answer.

She shrugs.

GABRIEL: I think we could all do with a drink, Dottie, if you wouldn't mind.

DOTTIE: Yeah, why not. Do the job while I still got it.

ANYA: I've got some money. Not much but – we could pay the mortgage for another month, buy ourselves a little more time?

VALERIE: How've you got money?

ANYA: You send me too much. I save it.

RAINEY: Bit late for that. Isn't it?

VALERIE: The auction is happening now.

GABRIEL: Not quite now, but certainly –

VALERIE looks at him.

GABRIEL: Shutting up.

VALERIE: It's done. It's too late.

RAINEY: You know I'm not feeling terribly well.

DOTTIE: Well there is this nasty bug going round.

DOTTIE helps RAINEY lower herself onto a couch.

ANYA pulls away from the group, CERI follows her.

ANYA: I feel like I knew this was going to happen. All this would be taken away from us.

CERI: And why d'you think you felt that?

ANYA: I'm a bit gloomy and depressive in my outlook?

CERI: Because you know it's wrong. For just your family to have all this.

ANYA: All that's going to happen is some other rich git will buy it. And not someone who loves the place like we do.

CERI: So if everyone else is stealing, you can too?

ANYA just looks at him.

CERI: And what does it feel like now? Now that what you knew was going to happen, is happening?

She fills with tears. Can't speak for a bit.

ANYA: It feels absolutely – [awful, heart-breaking]

And the sensation fades.

CERI: Okay. And what else?

ANYA: It feels sort of sad. And sort of a relief.

CERI: All this was yours. And that was lovely, but wrong. And now it's not yours. And that is sad, but right.

They sit.

ANYA: I think I might need some company tonight.

CERI: And I'll do, will I? For the night.

ANYA: You could. If you want. Or you could not.

CERI wants to walk away. Can't.

CERI: I am not like this.

LEWIS comes into the living room.

He is delighted.

LEWIS: It's done then.

RAINEY: Who bought it?

LEWIS: Me.

RAINEY: No: who bought the house, in the auction?

LEWIS: I did.

RAINEY: Gabriel can you get any sense out of him?

VALERIE: You said you couldn't afford to.

LEWIS: I couldn't, on my own. Got someone to come in with me.

RAINEY: You, have bought Bloumfield?

LEWIS: Yes, Rainey.

She looks at him a long time.

RAINEY: Well done.

VALERIE: You organised this partner quick.

LEWIS: One thing you learn in business: gotta have a plan B.

VALERIE: Selling the orchard was plan B.

LEWIS: 'S why I always got plan C as well. In case plan B doesn't come off.

She stares at him. Her suspicion evaporates. She throws her arms around him.

VALERIE: Thank you. Thank you so much.

LEWIS: It's better than the place going to a stranger.

VALERIE: Dottie, go and tell Anya – we're saved.

LEWIS: No no, hold on – that's not.

He frees himself from VALERIE.

LEWIS: I couldn't buy this place just to sit the way it is. That makes no sense. That's why you're in the trouble you are. I got someone to invest with me cos I had a plan. For how to make this place make money. We're gonna turn it into a hotel. Like really luxury place you know. Bloumfield Grove. Or Orchard Grove – we got ages to think of that.

VALERIE: And what about us?

LEWIS: Well, you've done so well running the place when it was basically just falling to bits – you could do brilliantly when it's got some investment behind it. So I thought, would you stay, and do the same thing. Be like – general manager.

VALERIE: Of my own house?

LEWIS: Well it's not, now. I mean I see what you're saying but –

She doesn't answer.

LEWIS: And I think the guests would really like, you know. The connection to the history of the place. Could be a real selling point.

VALERIE: So I'd be running round fetching and carrying for guests?

LEWIS: God no none of that. You'd be like, like I said – managing.

VALERIE stands.

Then goes.

LEWIS: No I know it's a lot to take in.

GABRIEL goes after her.

LEWIS turns to RAINEY.

LEWIS: You gonna be alright?

She doesn't answer.

LEWIS: Rainey.

No answer.

LEWIS: I'd better get into town then. See to the paperwork.

He turns to go.

RAINEY: Alun.

He stops.

RAINEY: After all these years, you finally screwed me. Was it worth it?

LEWIS: Ah good. I was starting to worry about you then.

He goes.

DOTTIE comes on with a flannel.

DOTTIE: There you are.

Puts in on RAINEY's head. RAINEY pushes it away.

RAINEY: Bloody hell that's freezing!

DOTTIE: I had it in the freezer. It'll help with the headache.

RAINEY: I haven't got a headache.

DOTTIE: No. But there's one in the post.

RAINEY: I feel like I'm gonna be sick again.

DOTTIE: Then you should be.

RAINEY: I don't want to be sick though.

DOTTIE: Then you should've had a very different kind of day. Now. Lie back.

RAINEY does as she's told.

DOTTIE very gently puts the flannel on RAINEY's forehead.

Tucks cushions in around her to make her comfortable.

Sits at her side.

After a while, DOTTIE begins very softly to sing. Something tender and sad – Myfanwy, or Gwahoddiad. Not something she does often. But beautiful.

Without moving from under her chilled flannel, RAINEY speaks.

RAINEY: You know they say the Welsh are good at singing.

She sits up.

RAINEY: Possibly some of them, but you my girl are more charming with your mouth shut. Though I'm sure that's not what the boys say.

DOTTIE: You know what, don't puke it up, I'd rather you suffered.

DOTTIE heads off –

– runs into GABRIEL, entering at speed.

GABRIEL: It's just been on the radio. On the news. I can't believe it.

RAINEY: What, for God's sake – but quietly...

GABRIEL: Argentina –

RAINEY: That is not quiet!

GABRIEL: *(Whispering forcefully.)* Argentina has invaded the Falklands.

DOTTIE: What?

GABRIEL: Argentina, has invaded the Falkland Islands.

DOTTIE: How the bloody hell did Argentina invade Scotland?

GABRIEL looks at her; understands.

GABRIEL: No no – not the Shetland Islands – the Falklands.

DOTTIE: Where the hell are they then?

GABRIEL: They're – just off Argentina basically.

DOTTIE: So, thousands and thousands of miles away?

GABRIEL: Yes I believe so.

DOTTIE: Sod that then.

She turns to RAINEY.

DOTTIE: I'm gonna get you all the aspirin we got in the house. If you're lucky it'll kill you.

RAINEY: That's very thoughtful.

GABRIEL waits for DOTTIE to be gone.

GABRIEL: Yes according to the reports it's all been very exciting, a dozen marines at the Governor's Mansion holding out against hundreds of Argentinian infantry, armour on the streets of Port Stanley –

RAINEY: Gabriel…

GABRIEL: What?

She just looks at him.

GABRIEL: Shutting up.

FIVE

The next day.

Coffee and breakfast things on the table.

ANYA comes on to find RAINEY still there.

ANYA: Have you been to bed?

RAINEY: Of course! Just up early.

ANYA's getting two cups of coffee.

RAINEY: Two cups I notice.

ANYA: …really need the caffeine.

RAINEY: Because your guest kept you up all night?

ANYA: Yes, alright.

RAINEY: He's a nice young man. You've done well.

ANYA: I could do better.

RAINEY: Well in theory. But have you, ever?

ANYA stares at her.

RAINEY: You know yesterday you mentioned you had some money spare.

ANYA: …yes.

RAINEY: And I wondered… could we give that –

ANYA: There's no point paying the mortgage now, that's not the [problem] – Lewis has / bought it –

RAINEY: Yes, *I know*, but could we pay it to Lewis, to get a little breathing space. A sort of rent. For a few months. For the summer. I'd love another summer.

ANYA: Well um –

RAINEY: With you and Val.

ANYA: – when I said I had some money I meant, I could get hold of some. If I had to.

They look at each other. VALERIE comes on, gets coffee, breaks the moment.

RAINEY: I see. Not to worry, darling.

ANYA: Mum was wondering, would Lewis let us stay a little while.

VALERIE: Well of course!

RAINEY: Because I was saying to Anya, I would love having one last summer with the both of you here.

VALERIE: Ah.

RAINEY: Ah?

VALERIE: I didn't realise you were talking about months and months.

RAINEY: What's one summer?

VALERIE: I know Lewis wants to start the building work as soon as he can. He's got architects coming today. But I'm sure he'd let you have a couple of weeks' grace.

RAINEY: But not the summer.

VALERIE: He can't afford to let the place sit idle.

RAINEY: Of course not, no.

DOTTIE enters.

DOTTIE: Coffee going down a treat, thought it might.

RAINEY: Dottie?

DOTTIE: Absolutely.

RAINEY: Could you pack my things?

DOTTIE: Things? You barely brought a bag.

RAINEY: Then that's what I'll take.

DOTTIE: Alright then.

DOTTIE picks up a few things as prelude to heading out.

VALERIE: You're going today?

RAINEY: There's no reason to dawdle.

ANYA: Don't bother Dot, she's bluffing.

RAINEY: Do bother, please Dottie.

DOTTIE: Well which?

ANYA: You just said you wanted to stay all summer.

RAINEY: But I can't. So now I'm saying something different.

ANYA: Alright. I'll run you to the station.

RAINEY: Thank you darling. Although – your car is a bit of a midden.

ANYA: Ah, here we go…

RAINEY: D'you think Lewis might take me, Val?

VALERIE: …he'll be glad to. *(To DOTTIE.)* Could you ring Lewis, ask him if he'll run Mum to the station.

DOTTIE: I could. And shall I, actually?

RAINEY: Yes, please.

DOTTIE goes.

ANYA: Alright fine.

ANYA goes off with the coffee cups.

VALERIE: Right then. I'd best pack too.

RAINEY: Where are you going?

VALERIE: You're going to sit drinking in a hotel till they kick you out on the streets. And then you're going to sit drinking on the streets / till you –

RAINEY: And you're going to stop me, are you?

VALERIE: I'm going to – no.

RAINEY: You have no idea what I might do. No idea at all.

GABRIEL enters.

GABRIEL: Morning all. Oh good, coffee.

VALERIE: Right. I'll get ready to go.

GABRIEL: Off for a shopping spree, is it?

RAINEY: That's right, yes. What a woman can't get in Carmarthen… she shall have to live without.

RAINEY's going.

VALERIE: At least tell him.

RAINEY: Nothing to tell.

She's gone.

VALERIE: She's not going shopping, she's going to catch a train. She said she was going shopping, because she couldn't be bothered to tell you herself.

GABRIEL: Oh. Oh well.

He takes a sip. DOTTIE returns.

GABRIEL: Probably best, all things considered. Go quick, if you're going.

VALERIE: And sneak off without saying good-bye?

GABRIEL takes a bite of some breakfast treat.

GABRIEL: *(As he eats.)* We've been brother and sister half a century. Through awful things. D'you think saying 'good-bye' makes any difference?

A slurp of coffee.

GABRIEL: Not a jot.

VALERIE goes.

GABRIEL: Dottie my love, I wondered if we might have a chat.

GABRIEL is eating throughout.

DOTTIE: Well I've got more to do this morning than could be achieved by a small army in week, but – I'm gonna be out of a job end of the month so sod it.

GABRIEL: And that's actually what I wanted to talk to you about. Your future.

DOTTIE: Oh God let's not. Take it a day at a time me.

GABRIEL: As you know my position has improved, lately –

DOTTIE: How's that?

GABRIEL: Got a new job.

DOTTIE: Oh yes! Just hard to, imagine you somehow / doing a –

GABRIEL: So as you know I have this rather lovely house myself, not the equal of Bloumfield by any means but still, and I am a solvent individual, and it's just me, no children, and of course your position here will shortly be –

DOTTIE: Gone.

GABRIEL: – yes, quite, so I wondered – how would you feel about it?

DOTTIE: About coming to you?

GABRIEL: We get on, don't we?

DOTTIE: We have a giggle, yeah.

GABRIEL: And I think that's really really important. That the daily business of living is / full of laughter

DOTTIE: I suppose it's just – I've been a house-keeper donkeys years now, I think I might fancy something different.

GABRIEL: And yes of course there'd be an element of house-keeping, but um –

He comes to a stop.

DOTTIE: But um what?

GABRIEL: I'm not asking you to be my house-keeper.

DOTTIE: What are you asking me then?

GABRIEL: To be my… I suppose companion.

DOTTIE goes to speak –

– can't.

GABRIEL: I wouldn't make any excessive demands upon you. Only what's normal. And only… in the fullness of time.

DOTTIE: I'm sorry I'm not [sure I understand] –

GABRIEL: I think there's a spark. Isn't there?

DOTTIE: …no.

GABRIEL: You flirt with me outrageously!

DOTTIE: You're my boss's brother.

GABRIEL: So there's no – attraction?

DOTTIE: Between you and me?

GABRIEL: Yes.

DOTTIE: You and me?

GABRIEL: *Yes.*

DOTTIE: You… and me?

GABRIEL: Well I say, I've, I don't know what you're [trying to say] – and I've a lovely home, man of some standing, man of some means, before long. Never killed anyone.

DOTTIE: My boyfriend, yeah?

GABRIEL: Gosh I didn't know you / had a –

DOTTIE: Cos it's none of your business but – his thigh is so rock hard, when you bite it, if you bite hard enough, your teeth just break. Like that. Teeth and blood in your mouth.

GABRIEL: Why on earth would you be biting his thigh?

DOTTIE: Gabriel mun.

She begins to clear things away.

DOTTIE: We'll miss your kind, when you're gone. Not straight off but, after twenty thirty years. When we've had time to forget what you were actually like.

She takes plates away. Goes.

GABRIEL has a new idea.

GABRIEL: Well alright, what about, just as my housekeeper. What about that? Dottie?

But she's gone.

GABRIEL: That's alright, I'll be fine.

He finds something else to eat. Takes a bite.

Elsewhere: ANYA and CERI. Drinking coffee. Staring at each other.

CERI: …you.

ANYA: Yes.

CERI: You're too much.

ANYA: People do say.

CERI: You see that it's better, don't you?

ANYA nods.

CERI: How's it better?

ANYA: If the place becomes a hotel, it's not just us that get to enjoy it. It's lots of people.

CERI: Lewis converts the place so lots of people can use it, not just one family. And then after capitalism – it becomes some kind of facility, where anyone can come and stay if they need a little break somewhere beautiful.

ANYA: That's a hotel.

CERI: Difference is it'll be for everyone. Distributed according to need.

ANYA: You should do this Enterprise Allowance thing.

CERI: Well I can't.

ANYA: I've got money. I'll give you a thousand pounds.

CERI stares at her.

ANYA: Why not?

CERI: What does that mean, if you give me a thousand quid. For us?

ANYA: It means I own you and can have you whenever I want.

CERI: I can't just take your money.

ANYA: If you were some rich kid you would in a second.

CERI: *(Attempts a posh accent.)* Now I won't say a word against poor people, but sometimes aren't they a drag, making such a big deal out of money, when it's just – it's just *paper...*

ANYA: Well, you are being a drag. And this *(His sarcasm.)* especially, is a massive drag. Because actually it is just paper, to me. It doesn't have to mean anything between us. Unless you let it.

CERI gets up, getting ready to leave.

CERI: I can't take money off you.

ANYA: Just going to be a dolie, forever.

CERI: Never gonna be able to keep you in furs and fine wine...

ANYA: Ceri love: you were never in the running.

CERI goes to the living room.

Looks for something. Can't find it.

DOTTIE enters with a coffee pot.

CERI: Ah, was looking for that.

DOTTIE fills him up.

CERI: So what for you now?

She shrugs.

CERI: Been here donkeys' years haven't you?

DOTTIE: Since school.

CERI: So that's all your life. You've just worked here – and now it's going. Christ are you alright?

DOTTIE: Course. I mean I seen it coming. I had other offers already.

CERI: Anything interesting?

DOTTIE: Interesting's the word...

ANYA enters.

ANYA: What're you two conspiring about?

CERI: Did you realise / Dottie's –

DOTTIE: Your mum's really off, by the way.

ANYA: No she's not.

DOTTIE: Lewis said he'd be here now.

ANYA: Right now, or now as in now after he's been to Ha'fordwest to pick up feed?

DOTTIE: Now as in driving straight here, now.

ANYA: Well okay. I'm having a bath.

ANYA goes.

CERI: They told you, how much longer you got?

DOTTIE: They've hardly got a clue themselves.

CERI: So what're you supposed to do?

DOTTIE: I'll be alright, don't worry about me.

CERI: And it must be sad.

DOTTIE: Must it.

DOTTIE gets on with something.

CERI: Leaving the place you've always been. Or leaving the people.

DOTTIE: 'S only Val's still here. I'll see her around.

CERI: Yeah but you and Rainey.

DOTTIE: What?

CERI: She's known you since you were a girl.

That's not what he meant to say.

DOTTIE: Then I've probably known her long enough.

Off CERI's look –

DOTTIE: What?

CERI: Always seems like you're thick as thieves.

DOTTIE: Well.

CERI just watches as she gets on with her task.

DOTTIE: Well she's my boss, isn't she.

DOTTIE carries on. CERI goes for some sugar or milk.

DOTTIE stops what she's doing.

DOTTIE: When he knew it was the end my dad, he wouldn't stay in the hospital. He was an awkward sod, he wanted to come home. He had cancer, all through him. My mum stayed home to nurse him but he wouldn't, you know – go. Stubborn sod too. And thing is we had to eat. And in the end Mum had to go to work. So I came out of school. And I stayed with him. Had to give him his medicine, for the pain. Except that last day, it was too much. He was screaming. And I was supposed to give him the medicine – but I was too scared to go near. So I shut the door. Hid in the kitchen. And that's what I remember. A monster screaming at me. My mum had to go to work that day, and she went to work the next day too. Took me with her. That's when I started here. Everybody loses people. Rich cow like Rainey runs off, drinks herself senseless for a decade and she gets away with it. You're poor you just have to carry on. Like what you lost was nothing. Fuck her grief.

LEWIS walks in. Right into the middle of the room.

Has a sense he's walked in on something. Looks at them book.

LEWIS: Sorry have I –

DOTTIE: Boots!

LEWIS: Sorry what?

DOTTIE: Muddy boots, on my clean floor.

LEWIS: I think it's *my* floor.

DOTTIE: I bloody swept it!

LEWIS: Alright, alright…

LEWIS pads back to the entrance, pulls off his boots.

DOTTIE leaves.

CERI: How're you this morning?

LEWIS: Bit of a sore head.

CERI: I bet.

LEWIS: I still can't –

He looks round the place.

LEWIS: This was the first place round here to get electric. It was just a diesel genny to run the milking machine and they'd run half a dozen lamps off it at night. But you'd see it. Golden light blazing out over the valley, while we were huddled round oil lamps.

CERI: Ah, the smell of paraffin! Can't beat it. Kids today with their superglue, they don't know what they're missing.

LEWIS: You think the people in a grand place like this are better, cos they're here. But actually – they're just here. All it takes is you get them out –

CERI: – and they're as useless as you are.

LEWIS smiles.

LEWIS: How is life on the dole.

CERI: Very relaxing thanks.

LEWIS: She's a cracking girl, Anya. She's a bit – you know, for you...

CERI: I don't know, as it happens.

LEWIS: She's gonna do better, isn't she.

CERI: I was awake a bit in the night, you know what I heard on the World Service?

LEWIS: You were cwtshed up in bed with a twenty year old, and you were listening to the World Service? That's not what I'd've been doing.

CERI: Well I'm in bed with twenty year olds a bit more often than you are, Lew, so it's not such a big thing for me.

ANYA wanders on.

CERI: *(To ANYA.)* Hiya love, you alright?

ANYA: Yeah fine.

CERI: Quick bath.

ANYA: Yeah I didn't actually – *(She stops.)* I think Mum's packing?

CERI: Packing to go?

ANYA: She's dashing around putting things, more or less at random, into a case. Do you think she is going?

CERI: I have no way of knowing, do I?

LEWIS: Tell you what kid, when you wanna join the working week, you let me know. Cos you're bright enough, you could make something of yourself – but you'd rather sit on the dole, sniping.

CERI: How many cliches was that in one sentence?

LEWIS: They're cliches –

CERI: – cos they're true, there's another one.

LEWIS: Every penny you spend comes from people like me working our guts out. And you know it.

CERI: I'm not on the dole any more.

ANYA pricks up her ears at this.

LEWIS: You and Gabriel got a job the same week? Britain's working again!

CERI: Actually I'm setting up myself.

LEWIS: Setting up what?

CERI: A record label.

ANYA goes over to him. Takes his hand. Brings it to her mouth, kisses it.

LEWIS takes this in.

LEWIS: You're setting up *a business*? That is – oh Ceri mun. That is / the best thing –

He is genuinely pleased; and also finds it hilarious.

CERI: Yeah well you're still paying for it mate. It's all a government scheme.

ANYA: It's going to be brilliant. I'm really proud of you.

LEWIS: What's scheme's that?

CERI: Enterprise Allowance.

LEWIS: Don't you have to have a grand to get started on that?

CERI: …yeah.

LEWIS: Where are you getting a grand?

CERI: Anya's lending it me.

ANYA: I didn't say lend, you can have it.

LEWIS: Good of her.

ANYA: It's just sitting in my bank account otherwise.

LEWIS: Still, it's good of –

He stops.

LEWIS: Was that your mum calling you?

ANYA looks – she heard nothing. Because there was nothing.

ANYA: This'll be the excuses starting…

ANYA goes off.

LEWIS: You're gonna take money off that girl?

CERI: She offered.

LEWIS: She's a bloody child!

CERI: No, she's not…

LEWIS: She's a child, and she's thinks she's in love with you –

CERI: She really doesn't!

LEWIS: I'll lend it you if you need it that bad.

CERI: And I'd never hear the end of it.

LEWIS: I love that a Trot like you's starting a business, that's enough for me. Man to man now, I wouldn't say a word.

CERI: Man to man?

LEWIS: Man to boy then.

CERI: And how do I explain to Anya I've suddenly got a thousand pounds? Counted the coppers under the settee cushions and guess what –

LEWIS: Say you grew some balls and went to the bank. You feel proud of yourself, taking money off a girl?

CERI doesn't answer.

LEWIS: Cos I'll tell you this – you let a woman pay your way, that's it. She might keep you around, she might play with you – but you're not a man to her. You're a pet. And one day a man will come along…

CERI smiles.

LEWIS: What's so funny?

CERI: You know what it was, I heard on the World Service last night?

LEWIS: More a Radio 2 bloke. Like a tune if I'm up in the night.

CERI: Oh yeah? What tunes d'you like Lew?

LEWIS knows to say anything will be to invite mockery.

LEWIS: Can't remember.

CERI: What it said on the World Service was, we used to have a warship that patrolled round the Falklands, to keep the Argentinians off.

LEWIS: We used to.

CERI: Yeah. Used to. And do you know who got rid of it?

LEWIS can guess, but isn't going to play along.

CERI: Maggie. Thatcher.

LEWIS: I dunno how one ship could've / held off an –

CERI: Cos the British public will put up with a lot. Three million unemployed. Riots all over the country. That they'll take. But let sacred British territory fall – and to the bloody Argentinians! Oh no. No chance. It's a thousand years since we got invaded. And who let it happen? Maggie Thatcher. Your Iron Lady's finished mate. And you know it.

LEWIS: Like I say, anytime you want a job / I can give you one –

RAINEY enters, coat over her arm, handbag and a small case and immediately talks over CERI. ANYA following her.

RAINEY: Lewis, excellent. Thanks so much for this.

ANYA: Look.

She means, that RAINEY seems to be about to leave.

CERI: I can see.

RAINEY's hovering around the dresser, looking for something.

RAINEY: Ah! There we are.

LEWIS: What's that?

ANYA: It's a ceramic walrus.

LEWIS looks to CERI; CERI has no idea either.

LEWIS: Fair play.

RAINEY opens her case, finds an item of clothing to wrap the walrus in, packs it away.

ANYA: I think she's going. *(To LEWIS.)* Can we come with you?

LEWIS: Yeah, if you two fancy the spin –

ANYA: I want to see if she actually gets on the train.

LEWIS: Actually if Val comes there won't be room in the car.

ANYA: Fine, we'll go in mine.

RAINEY: Gosh, am I getting a convoy?

ANYA: The departing usually do.

RAINEY offers ANYA her case.

RAINEY: Be a darling and take this to the car for me?

ANYA takes the case; hands it off to CERI.

CERI takes the case. Goes.

RAINEY: Right then. Where's Dottie?

ANYA: I don't know. Dottie!

No response.

ANYA: DOTTIE!

No response.

ANYA: She's not coming.

RAINEY: That's alright, I'll find her.

RAINEY goes.

ANYA: She won't be able to find Dottie now. Or there'll be something else she absolutely must have she can't lay her hands on. Or – you'll see. There's no way she's going to –

ANYA stands. Sits. Gets up again.

ANYA: I can't stand this, I'm going to wait in the car.

ANYA goes off, in the same direction as CERI.

Elsewhere – RAINEY finds DOTTIE.

RAINEY: Hello.

DOTTIE sighs.

DOTTIE: Yes, what?

RAINEY: Well I'll be off then.

DOTTIE: See you.

RAINEY: I really am.

DOTTIE looks at her.

DOTTIE: Well we'll see, [won't we]

DOTTIE sees.

DOTTIE: Are you sure?

RAINEY shakes her head.

Then –

– takes a chain from round her neck. On it a wedding band.

RAINEY: I want you to have this.

DOTTIE says nothing.

RAINEY: I kept his ring at first to remind me that however useless I was, I was never as weak as him. But the truth is, if he'd said to me Rainey let's go for a spin in the car, I'd've got in. I'd've known. And I'd've got in. So really – Anyway it's nothing now. But it's worth a few bob, so –

She offers the ring, still on the chain.

DOTTIE: I can't.

RAINEY: You need the money. And you more than deserve it.

DOTTIE: I can't take that from you.

RAINEY: Please.

DOTTIE: No.

RAINEY: When things were terrible, just afterwards –

DOTTIE: Rainey.

RAINEY: You were the only one I had and it means a great deal to me that you / take it –

DOTTIE: I can't alright because –

DOTTIE looks at her –

– crumbles.

RAINEY steps forward; presses the gift into her hand.

RAINEY: Thank you.

RAINEY wants to hug her, waits for a signal to move in.

Doesn't get one.

And then does. RAINEY hugs her.

RAINEY: Thank you. Thank you darling girl.

RAINEY goes.

In the living room –

LEWIS: How long you gonna up there with her in London?

VALERIE: Depends. We'll see how long she takes.

LEWIS: Right.

He walks to the window.

LEWIS: I still can't get over it.

VALERIE's watching him, expecting something. He's taking in his new possession.

VALERIE: We will get round to making it official, won't we?

LEWIS: Well it's all –

He looks at her, knows what she means.

LEWIS: You and me?

She nods.

LEWIS: Of course we will.

VALERIE: Good, 'cause it'd be a pity to –

LEWIS: No, no. We're a good team.

They look at each other.

LEWIS: D'you want to now?

VALERIE: Right now?

LEWIS: I haven't got a ring or anything but we don't need that really. We could just say to each other, right now, and that would be enough.

VALERIE: Tell you what: let's take our time, do it properly.

LEWIS: Probably for the best, yeah. Bound to want a bit of fuss, aren't you.

VALERIE: Doesn't every girl.

LEWIS: Cos you're not the type to want fuss normally but like you say there are some things –

VALERIE: Lewis –

LEWIS: What?

VALERIE: What if I don't come back?

They look at each other.

RAINEY walks in, GABRIEL with her, putting on a coat.

RAINEY: Alright then. Alright.

RAINEY picks up her own coat.

RAINEY: Best be heading off, if we're going to get that train.

LEWIS: Not another one for six hours.

RAINEY: Yes, don't want to risk it.

RAINEY just stands there.

LEWIS: So shall we go?

RAINEY: Absolutely.

She doesn't move.

RAINEY: Could I just have a minute, with my brother?

LEWIS: Course.

LEWIS heads off. VALERIE hesitates.

RAINEY: Yes, I'll be with you in a moment.

VALERIE and LEWIS go to leave.

LEWIS realises he has no boots on.

He starts to put his boots on.

Realises everyone is watching him.

LEWIS: I'll just be a second now.

Struggles with the laces.

LEWIS: Tricky doing your laces with people watching you.

VALERIE: Isn't it.

He stands, finally.

LEWIS: See you at the car.

They go.

GABRIEL: Well here we are then.

They look at each other. Suddenly –

GABRIEL: Oh, by the way –

He searches in his pockets. Finds what he's looking for.

Gets out RAINEY's wedding ring, on its chain.

GABRIEL: Dottie gave me this for you. Said you'd dropped it
somewhere. Knew you'd hate to lose it.

RAINEY takes the ring.

RAINEY: How very good of her.

GABRIEL: Yes, she is good, isn't she. It'll be odd not [having
her around] – well yes.

GABRIEL falls silent.

RAINEY: Is this it?

GABRIEL: It doesn't have to be. You could have another week
or two.

RAINEY: And what's the use of that?

GABRIEL: It's time. It's more time.

RAINEY: No. This is it. This is it now.

She looks round.

RAINEY: This is it. This is it all.

She gets a little panicky.

RAINEY: I'm trying to think of it. I'm trying to think of it all. And there's too much.

GABRIEL: There's a lifetime.

RAINEY: There's more than that. There's all of us. There's us – we were children. We were brother and sister. Every day, I spent with you. And now –

GABRIEL: There's everyone that went before.

RAINEY: And I knew. I knew it would be the golden time, when the kids were tiny. I didn't know how quick – I can see them all. I can see Jo, Anya, Mum, Dad – you. Me. All of us.

VALERIE calls from off.

VALERIE: *(Off.)* God's sake Mum we're going to miss that bloody train!

GABRIEL: Thank you darling!

He turns back to RAINEY.

GABRIEL: Shall we stay. Another week. Perhaps you've hurried this –

RAINEY: Just let me have one minute alone. Would you do that?

GABRIEL: Of course!

He doesn't move.

RAINEY: Just one minute then.

GABRIEL touches her arm; goes.

RAINEY stands. Looks at her watch.

RAINEY: One minute. One minute. I'll take what I can in one minute and then I'll go. But now I can't think of anything. I'm just thinking of numbers. Fifty-nine, fifty-eight, fifty-seven –

She looks round the place.

RAINEY: No. No.

She's silent a moment. And then –

RAINEY: I'm so sorry. But I had to. I had to.

She picks up her handbag.

Goes.

Silence.

And then the room tone gets louder: the tick of the clock, wind against the window.

DOTTIE comes in. Surveys the mess of breakfast. Sighs.

Picks up three or four plates, tipping food remains on the top one, stacking them. Picks up coffee pot in her free hand.

Goes.

Now the sounds of the orchard fill the room. Bird song, leaves in the breeze, branches creaking.

A toy truck rolls on to the stage.

It sits there.

And then –

– a little boy, nine or ten, runs on.

He picks up the truck.

Rolls it one way, catches it, then rolls it back the other direction.

The noise of the orchard gives way to the sound of waves rushing to the shore.

The boy picks up his toy, stands. Speaks, absent-minded.

BOY: Mummy?

He calls again, as if he thought he heard an answer but wasn't sure.

BOY: Mummy?

Still no answer. Worried now, he shouts.

BOY: MUMMY!

To black. And wave after wave after wave, crashing against the shore.

END